CONTENTS

1. Corasmin and the Parrots   5

2. Walk to Huayapa   11

3. The Mozo   25

4. Market Day   35

5. Indians and Entertainment   41

6. Dance of the Sprouting Corn   51

7. The Hopi Snake Dance   56

8. A Little Moonshine with Lemon   74

MORNINGS IN MEXICO
D H LAWRENCE

ISBN: 978-1508471035

www.dogstailbooks.co.uk

1 - CORASMIN AND THE PARROTS

One says Mexico: one means, after all, one little town away South in the Republic: and in this little town, one rather crumbly adobe house built round two sides of a garden *patio*: and of this house, one spot on the deep, shady veranda facing inwards to the trees, where there are an onyx table and three rocking-chairs and one little wooden chair, a pot with carnations, and a person with a pen. We talk so grandly, in capital letters, about Morning in Mexico. All it amounts to is one little individual looking at a bit of sky and trees, then looking down at the page of his exercise book.

It is a pity we don't always remember this. When books come out with grand titles, like *The Future of America*, or *The European Situation*, it's a pity we don't immediately visualize a thin or a fat person, in a chair or in bed, dictating to a bob-haired stenographer or making little marks on paper with a fountain pen.

Still, it is morning, and it is Mexico. The sun shines. But then, during the winter, it always shines. It is pleasant to sit out of doors and write, just fresh enough and just warm enough. But then it is Christmas next week, so it ought to be just right.

There is a little smell of carnations, because they are the nearest thing. And there is a resinous smell of ocote wood, and a smell of coffee, and a faint smell of leaves, and of Morning, and even of Mexico. Because when all is said and done, Mexico has a faint, physical scent of her own, as each human being has. And this is a curious, inexplicable scent, in which there are resin and perspiration and sunburned earth and urine among other things.

And cocks are still crowing. The little mill where the natives have their own corn ground is puffing rather languidly. And because some women are talking in the entrance-way, the two tame parrots in the trees have started to whistle.

The parrots, even when I don't listen to them, have an extraordinary effect on me. They make my diaphragm convulse with little laughs, almost mechanically. They are a quite commonplace pair of green birds, with bits of bluey red, and round, disillusioned eyes, and heavy, overhanging noses. But they listen intently. And they reproduce. The pair whistle now like Rosalino, who is sweeping the *patio* with a twig broom; and yet it is so unlike him, to be whistling full vent, when any of us is around, that one looks at him to see. And the moment one sees him, with his black head bent rather drooping and hidden as he sweeps, one laughs.

The parrots whistle exactly like Rosalino, only a little more so. And this little-more-so is extremely sardonically funny. With their sad old long-jowled faces and their flat disillusioned eyes, they reproduce Rosalino and a little-more-so without moving a muscle. And Rosalino, sweeping the *patio* with his twig broom, scraping and tittering leaves into little heaps, covers himself more and more with the cloud of his own obscurity. He doesn't rebel. He is powerless. Up goes the wild, sliding Indian whistle into the morning, very powerful, with an immense energy seeming to drive behind it. And always, always a little more than life-like.

Then they break off into a cackling chatter, and one knows they are shifting their clumsy legs, perhaps hanging on with their beaks and clutching with their cold, slow claws, to climb to a higher bough, like rather raggedy green buds climbing to the sun. And suddenly the penetrating, demonish mocking voices:

'Perro! Oh, Perro! Perr-rro! Oh, Perr-rro! Perro!'

They are imitating somebody calling the dog. *Perro* means dog. But that any creature should be able to pour such a suave, prussic-acid sarcasm over the voice of a human being calling a dog, is incredible. One's diaphragm chuckles involuntarily. And one thinks: *Is it possible?* Is it possible that we are so absolutely, so innocently, so *ab ovo* ridiculous?

And not only is it possible, it is patent. We cover our heads in confusion.

Now they are yapping like a dog: exactly like Corasmin. Corasmin is a little fat, curly white dog who was lying in the sun a minute ago, and has now come into the veranda shade, walking with slow resignation, to lie against the wall near-by my chair. 'Yap-yap-yap! Wouf! Wouf! Yapyapyapyap!' go the parrots, exactly like Corasmin when some stranger comes into the *zaguán*, Corasmin and a little-more-so.

With a grin on my face I look down at Corasmin. And with a silent, abashed resignation in his yellow eyes, Corasmin looks up at me, with a touch of reproach. His little white nose is sharp, and under his eyes there are dark marks, as under the eyes of one who has known much trouble. All day he does nothing but walk resignedly out of the sun, when the sun gets too hot, and out of the shade, when the shade gets too cool. And bite ineffectually in the region of his fleas.

Poor old Corasmin: he is only about six, but resigned, unspeakably resigned. Only not humble. He does not kiss the rod. He rises in spirit above it, letting his body lie.

'Perro! Oh, Perr-rro! Perr-rro! Perr-rr-rro!!' shriek the parrots, with that strange penetrating, antediluvian malevolence that seems to make even the trees prick their ears. It is a sound that penetrates one straight at the diaphragm, belonging to the ages before brains were invented. And Corasmin pushes his sharp little nose into his bushy tail, closes his eyes because I am grinning, feigns to sleep and then, in an orgasm of self-consciousness, starts up to bite in the region of his fleas.

'Perr-rro! Perr-rro!' And then a restrained, withheld sort of yapping. The fiendish rolling of the Spanish 'r', malevolence rippling out of all the vanished spiteful aeons. And following it, the small, little-curly-dog sort of yapping. They can make their voices so devilishly small and futile, like a little curly dog. And follow it up with that ringing malevolence that swoops up the ladders of the sunbeams right to the stars, rolling the Spanish 'r'.

Corasmin slowly walks away from the veranda, his head drooped, and flings himself down in the sun. No! He gets up again, in an agony of self-control, and scratches the earth loose a little, to soften his lie. Then flings himself down again.

Invictus! The still-unconquered Corasmin! The sad little white curly pendulum oscillating ever slower between the shadow and the sun.

In the fell clutch of circumstance I have not winced nor cried aloud, Under the bludgeonings of chance My head is bloody, but unbowed.

But that is human bombast, and a little too ridiculous even for Corasmin. Poor old Corasmin's clear yellow eyes! He is going to be master of his own soul, under all the vitriol those parrots pour over him. But he's not going to throw out his chest in a real lust of self-pity. That belongs to the next cycle of evolution.

I wait for the day when the parrots will start throwing English at us, in the pit of our stomachs. They cock their heads and listen to our gabble. But so far they haven't got it. It puzzles them. Castilian, and Corasmin, and Rosalino come more natural.

Myself, I don't believe in evolution, like a long string hooked on to a First Cause, and being slowly twisted in unbroken continuity through the ages. I prefer to believe in what the Aztecs called Suns: that is, Worlds successively created and destroyed. The sun itself convulses, and the worlds go out like so many candles when somebody coughs in the middle of them. Then subtly, mysteriously, the sun convulses again, and a new set of worlds begins to flicker alight.

This pleases my fancy better than the long and weary twisting of the rope of Time and Evolution, hitched on to the revolving hook of a First Cause. I like to think of the whole show going bust, *bang!*--and nothing but bits of chaos flying about. Then out of the dark, new little twinklings reviving from nowhere, nohow.

I like to think of the world going pop! when the lizards had grown too unwieldy, and it was time they were taken down a peg or two. Then the little humming birds beginning to spark in the darkness, and a whole succession of birds shaking themselves clean of the dark matrix, flamingoes rising upon one leg like dawn commencing, parrots shrieking about at midday, *almost* able to talk, then peacocks unfolding at evening like the night with stars. And apart from these little pure birds, a lot of unwieldy skinny-necked monsters bigger than crocodiles, barging through the mosses; till it was time to put a stop to them. When someone mysteriously touched the button, and the sun went bang, with smithereens of birds bursting in all directions. On a few parrots' eggs and peacocks' eggs and eggs of flamingoes smuggling in some safe nook, to hatch on the next Day, when the animals arose.

Up reared the elephant, and shook the mud off his back. The birds watched him in sheer stupefaction. What? *What in heaven's name is this wingless, beakless old perambulator?*

No good, oh birds! Curly, little white Corasmin ran yapping out of the undergrowth, the new undergrowth, till parrots, going white at the gills, flew off into the ancientest recesses. Then the terrific neighing of the wild horse was heard in the twilight for the first time, and the bellowing of lions through the night.

And the birds were sad. What is this? they said. A whole vast gamut of new noises. A universe of new voices.

Then the birds under the leaves hung their heads and were dumb. No good our making a sound, they said. We are superseded.

The great big, booming, half-naked birds were blown to smithereens. Only the real little feathery individuals hatched out again and remained. This was a consolation. The larks and warblers cheered up, and began to say their little say, out of the old 'Sun', to the new sun. But the peacock, and the turkey, and the raven, and the parrot above all, they could not get over it. Because, in the old days of the Sun of Birds, they had been the big guns. The parrot had been the old boss of the flock. He was so clever.

Now he was, so to speak, up a tree. Nor dare he come down, because of the toddling little curly white Corasmin, and such-like, down below. He felt absolutely bitter. That wingless, beakless, featherless, curly, misshapen bird's nest of a Corasmin had usurped the face of the earth, waddling about, whereas his Grace, the heavy-nosed old Duke of a parrot, was forced to sit out of reach up a tree, dispossessed.

So, like the riff-raff up in the gallery at the theatre, aloft in the Paradiso of the vanished Sun, he began to whistle and jeer. *'Yap-yap!'* said his new little lordship of a Corasmin. 'Ye Gods!' cried the parrot. 'Hear him forsooth! *Yap-yap!* he says! Could anything be more imbecile? Yap-yap! Oh, Sun of the Birds, hark at that! *Yap-yap-yap!* Perro! *Perro! Perr-rro!* Oh, *Perr-rr-rro!*'

The parrot had found his cue. Stiff-nosed, heavy-nosed old duke of the birds, he wasn't going to give in and sing a new song, like those fool brown thrushes and nightingales. Let, them twitter and warble. The parrot was a gentleman of the old school. He was going to jeer now! Like an ineffectual old aristocrat.

'Oh, Perr-rro! Perr-rro-o-o-!'

The Aztecs say there have been four Suns and ours is the fifth. The first Sun, a tiger, or a jaguar, a night-spotted monster of rage, rose out of nowhere and swallowed it, with all its huge, mercifully forgotten insects along with it. The second Sun blew up in a great wind: that was when the big lizards must have collapsed. The third Sun burst in water, and drowned all the animals that were considered unnecessary, together with the first attempts at animal men.

Out of the floods rose our own Sun, and little naked man. 'Hello!' said the old elephant. 'What's that noise?' And he pricked his ears, listening to a new voice on the face of the earth. The sound of man, and *words* for the first time. Terrible, unheard-of sound. The elephant dropped his tail and ran into the deep jungle, and there stood looking down his nose.

But little white curly Corasmin was fascinated. *'Come on! Perro! Perro!'* called the naked two-legged one. And Corasmin, fascinated, said to himself: 'Can't stand out against that name. Shall have to go!' so off he trotted, at the heels of the naked one. Then came the horse, then the elephant, spell-bound at being given a name. The other animals ran for their lives and stood quaking.

In the dust, however, the snake, the oldest dethroned king of all, bit his tail once more and said to himself: *'Here's another! No end to these new lords of creation! But I'll bruise his heel! Just as I swallow the eggs of the parrot, and lick to the little Corasmin pups.'*

And in the branches, the parrot said to himself: *'Hello! What's this new sort of half-bird? Why, he's got Corasmin trotting at his heels! Must be a new sort of boss! Let's listen to him, and see if I can't take him off.'*

Perr-rro! Perr-rr-rro-oo! Oh, Perro!

The parrot had hit it.

And the monkey, cleverest of creatures, cried with rage when he heard men speaking. *'Oh, why couldn't I do it!'* he chattered. But no good, he belonged to the old Sun. So he sat and gibbered across the invisible gulf in time, which is the 'other dimension' that clever people gas about: calling it 'fourth dimension', as if you could measure it with a foot-rule, the same as the obedient other three dimensions.

If you come to think of it, when you look at the monkey, you are looking straight into the other dimension. He's got length and breadth and height all right, and he's in the same universe of Space and Time as you are. But there's another dimension. He's different, There's no rope of evolution linking him to you, like a navel string. No! Between you and him there's a cataclysm and another dimension. It's no good. You can't link him up. Never will. It's the other dimension.

He mocks at you and gibes at you and imitates you.

Sometimes he is even more *like* you than you are yourself. It's funny, and you laugh just a bit on wrong your face. It's the other dimension.

He stands in one Sun, you in another. He whisks his tail in one Day, you scratch your head in another. He jeers at you, and is afraid of you. You laugh at him and are frightened of him.

What's the length and the breadth, what's the height and the depths between you and me? says monkey.

You get out a tape-measure, and he flies into an obscene mockery of you.

It's the other dimension, put the tape-measure away, it won't serve.

'Perro! Oh, Perr-rro!' shrieks the parrot.

Corasmin looks up at me, as much as to say:

'It's the other dimension. There's no help for it. Let us agree about it.'

And I look down into his yellow eyes, and say:

'You're quite right, Corasmin, it's the other dimension. You and I, we admit it. But the parrot won't, and the monkey won't, and the crocodile won't, neither the earwig. They all wind themselves up and wriggle inside the cage of the other dimension, hating it. And those that have voices jeer, and those that have mouths bite, and the insects that haven't even mouths, they turn up their tails and nip with them, or sting, Just behaving according to their own dimension: which, for me, is the other dimension.'

And Corasmin wags his tail mildly, and looks at me with real wisdom in his eyes. He and I, we understand each other in the wisdom of the other dimension.

But the flat, saucer-eyed parrot won't have it. Just won't have it.

'Oh, Perro! Perr-rro! Perr-rro-o-o-o! Yap-yap-yap!'

And Rosalino, the Indian *mozo*, looks up at me with his eyes veiled by their own blackness. We won't have it either: he is hiding and repudiating. Between us also is the gulf of the other dimension, and he wants to bridge it with the foot-rule of the three-dimensional space. He knows it can't be done. So do I. Each of us knows the other knows.

But he can imitate me, even more than life-like. As the parrot can him. And I have to laugh at his *me*, a bit on the wrong side of my face, as he has to grin on the wrong side of his face when I catch his eye as the parrot is whistling *him*, With a grin, with a laugh we pay tribute to the other dimension. But Corasmin is wiser. In his clear, yellow eyes is the self-possession of full admission.

The Aztecs said this world, our Sun, would blow up from inside, in earthquakes. Then what will come, in the other dimension, when we are superseded?

2 - WALK TO HUAYAPA

Curious is the psychology of Sunday. Humanity enjoying itself is on the whole a dreary spectacle, and holidays are more disheartening than drudgery. One makes up one's mind: On Sundays and on *fiestas* I will stay at home, in the hermitage of the *patio*, with the parrots and Corasmin and the reddening coffee-berries. I will avoid the sight of people enjoying themselves'--or try to, without much success.

Then comes Sunday morning, with the peculiar looseness of its sunshine. And even if you keep mum, the better-half says: Let's go somewhere.

But, thank God, in Mexico at least one can't set off in the 'machine'. It is a question of a meagre horse and a wooden saddle; on a donkey; or what we called, as children, 'Shanks' pony'--the shanks referring discourteously to one's own legs.

We will go out of the town. Rosalino, we are going for a walk to San Felipe de las Aguas. Do you want to go, and carry the basket?'

'*Cómo no, Señor?*'

It is Rosalino's inevitable answer, as inevitable as the parrot's 'Perro?' '*Cone no, Señor?*'--'How not, Señor?'

The *Norte*, the north-wind, was blowing last night, rattling the worm-chewed window-frames.

'Rosalino, I am afraid you will be cold in the night.'

'*Cómo no, Señor?*'

'Would you like a blanket?'

'*Cómo no, Señor?*'

'With this you will be warm?'

'*Cómo no, Señor?*'

But the morning is perfect; in a moment we are clear out of the town. Most towns in Mexico, saving the capital, end in themselves, at once. As if they had been lowered from heaven in a napkin, and deposited, rather foreign, upon the wild plain. So we walk round the wall of the church and the huge old monastery enclosure that is now barracks for the scrap-heap soldiery, and at once there are the hills.

'I will lift up my eyes unto the hills, whence cometh my strength.' At least one can always do *that*, in Mexico. In a stride, the town passes away. Before us lies the gleaming, pinkish-ochre of the valley flat, wild and exalted with sunshine. On the left, quite near, bank the stiffly pleated mountains, all the foot-hills, that press savannah-coloured into the savannah of the valley. The mountains are clothed smokily with pine, *ocote*, and, like a woman in a gauze *rebozo*, they rear in a rich blue fume that is almost cornflower-blue in the clefts. It is their characteristic that they are darkest blue at the top. Like some splendid lizard with a wavering, royal-blue crest down the ridge of his back, and pale belly, and soft, pinky-fawn claws, no the plain.

Between the pallor of the claws, a dark spot of trees, and white dots of a church with twin towers. Further away, along the foot-hills, a few scattered trees, white dot and stroke of .a hacienda, and a green, green square of sugar-cane. Further off still, at the mouth of a cleft of a canyon, a dense little green patch of trees, and two spots of proud church.

'Rosalino, which is San Felipe?'

'*Quien sabe, Señor?* says Rosalino, looking at the villages; beyond the sun of the savannah with black, visionless eyes. In his voice is the inevitable flat resonance of aloofness, touched with resignation, as if to say: It is not becoming to a man to know these things.--Among the Indians it is not becoming to know anything, not even one's own name.

Rosalino is a mountain boy, an Indian from a village two days' walk away. But he has been two years in the little city, and has learnt his modicum of Spanish.

'Have you never been to any of these villages?'

'No, *Señor*, I never went.'

'Didn't you want to?'

'*Cómo no, Señor?*

The Americans would call him a dumb-bell.

We decide for the farthest speck of a village in a dark spot of trees. It lies so magical, alone, tilted in the fawn-pink slope, again as if the dark-green napkin with a few white tiny buildings had been lowered from heaven and left, there at the foot of the mountains, with the deep groove of a canyon slanting in behind. So alone and, as it were, detached from the world in which it lies, a spot.

Nowhere more than in Mexico does human life become isolated, external to its surroundings, and cut off tinily from the environment. Even as you come across the plain to a big city like Guadalajara, and see the twin towers of the cathedral peering around in loneliness like two lost birds side by side on a moor, lifting their white heads to look around in the wilderness, your heart gives a clutch, feeling the pathos, the isolated tininess of human effort. As for building a church with one tower only, it is unthinkable. There must be two towers, to keep each other company in this wilderness world.

The morning is still early, the brilliant sun does not burn too much. Tomorrow is the shortest day. The savannah valley is shadeless, spotted only with the thorny ravel of mesquite bushes. Down the trail that has worn grooves in the turf--the rock is near the surface--occasional donkeys with a blue-hooded woman perched on top come tripping in silence, twinkling, a shadow. Just occasional women taking a few vegetables to market. Practically no men. It is Sunday.

Rosalino, prancing behind with the basket, plucks up his courage to speak to one of the women passing on a donkey. 'Is that San Felipe where we are going?'--'No, that is not San Felipe.'--'What, then, is it called?'--'It is called Huayapa.'--'Which, then, is San Felipe?'--That one'--and she points to her right.

They have spoken to each other in half-audible, crushed tones, as they always do, the woman on the donkey and the woman with her on foot swerving away from the basket-carrying Rosalino. They all swerve away from us, as if we were potential bold brigands. It really gets one's pecker up. The presence of the *Señora* only half reassures them. For the *Señora*, in a plain hat of bluey-green woven grass, and a dress of white cotton with black squares on it, is almost a monster of unusualness. *Prophet art thou, bird, or devil?* the women seem to say, as they look at her with keen black eyes. I think they choose to decide she is more of the last.

The women look at the woman, the men look at the man. And always with that same suspicious, inquiring, wondering look, the same with which Edgar Allan Poe must have looked at his momentous raven:

'*Prophet art thou, bird, or devil?*'

Devil, then, to please you! one longs to answer, in a tone of *Nevermore*.

Ten o'clock, and the sun getting hot. Not a spot of shade, apparently, from here to Huayapa. The blue getting thinner on the mountains, and an indiscernible vagueness, of too much light, descending on the plain.

The road suddenly dips into a little crack, where runs a creek. This again is characteristic of these parts of America. Water keeps out of sight. Even the biggest rivers, even the tiny brooks. You look across a plain on which the light sinks down, and you think: Dry! Dry! Absolutely dry! You travel along, and suddenly come to a crack in the earth, and a little stream is running in a little walled-in valley bed, where is a half-yard of green turf, and bushes, the *palo-blanco* with leaves, and with big white flowers like pure white, crumpled cambric. Or you may come to a river a thousand feet below, sheer below you. But not in this valley. Only the stream.

'Shade!' says the *Señora*, subsiding under a steep bank.

'*Mucho calor!*' says Rosalino, taking off his extra-jaunty straw hat, and subsiding with the basket.

Down the slope are coming two women on donkeys. Seeing the terrible array of three people sitting under a bank, they pull up.

'*Adios!*' I say, with firm resonance.

'*Adios!*' says the *Señora*, with diffidence.

'*Adios!*' says the reticent Rosalino, his voice the shadow of ours.

'*Adios! Adios! Adios!*' say the women, in suppressed voices, swerving, neutral, past us on their self-contained, sway-eared asses.

When they have passed, Rosalino looks at me to see if I shall laugh. I give a little grin, and he gives me back a great explosive grin, throwing back his head in silence, opening his wide mouth and showing his soft pink tongue, looking along his cheeks with his saurian black eyes, in an access of *farouche* derision.

A great hawk, like an eagle, with white bars at the end of its wings, sweeps low over us, looking for snakes. One can hear the hiss of its pinions.

'*Gabilán,*' says Rosalino.

'What is it called in the *idioma?*'

'*Psia!*'--He makes the consonants explode and hiss.

'Ah!' says the *Señora*. 'One hears it in the wings. *Psia!*'

'Yes,' says Rosalino, with black eyes of incomprehension.

Down the creek, two native boys, little herdsmen, are bathing, stooping with knees together and throwing water over themselves, rising, gleaming dark coffee-red in the sun, wetly. They are very dark, and their wet heads are so black, they seem to give off a bluish light, like dark electricity.

The great cattle they are tending slowly plunge through the bushes, coming up-stream. At the place where the path fords the stream, a great ox stoops to drink. Comes a cow after him, and a calf, and a young bull. They all drink a little at the stream, their noses delicately touching the water. And then the young bull, horns abranch, stares fixedly, with some f the same Indian wonder-and-suspicion stare, at us sitting under the bank.

Up jumps the *Señora*, proceeds uphill, trying to save her dignity. The bull, slowly leaning into motion, moves across-stream like a ship unmoored. The bathing lad on the bank is hastily fastening his calico pantaloons round his ruddy-dark waist. The Indians have a certain rich physique, even this lad. He comes running short-step down the bank, uttering a birdlike whoop, his dark hair gleaming bluish. Stooping for a moment to select a stone, he runs athwart the hull, and aims the stone sideways at him. There is a thud, the ponderous, adventurous young animal swerves docilely round towards the stream. '*Becerro!*' cries the boy, in his bird-like, piping tone, selecting a stone to throw at the calf.

We proceed in the blazing sun up the slope. There is a white line at the foot of the trees. It looks like water running white over a weir. The supply of the town water comes this way. Perhaps this is a reservoir. A sheet of water I How lovely it would be, in this country, if there was a sheet of water with a stream running out of it! And those dense trees of Huayapa behind.

'What is that white, Rosalino? Is it water?'

'*El Blanco? Si, aqua, Señora,*' says that dumb-bell.

Probably, if the *Señora* had said: Is it milk? he would have replied in exactly the same way: *Si es leche, Señora!*--Yes, it's milk.

Hot, silent, walking only amidst a weight of light, out of which one hardly sees, we climb the spurs towards the dark trees. And as we draw nearer, the white slowly resolves into a broken, whitewashed wall.

'Oh!' exclaims the *Señora*, in real disappointment. 'It isn't water! it's a wall!'

'*Si, Señora. Es panteón.*' (They call a cemetery a *panteón*, down here.)

'It is a cemetery,' announces Rosalino, with a certain ponderous, pleased assurance, and without afterthought. But when I suddenly laugh at the absurdity, he also gives a sudden broken yelp of laughter.--They laugh as if it were against their will, as if it hurt them, giving themselves away.

It was nearing midday. At last we got into a shady lane, in which were puddles of escaped irrigation-water. The ragged semi-squalor of a half-tropical lane, with naked trees sprouting into spiky scarlet flowers, and bushes with biggish yellow flowers, sitting rather wearily on their stems, led to the village.

We were entering Huayapa. *la Calle de las Minas*, said an old notice. *la Calle de las Minas*, said a new, brand-new notice, as if in confirmation. *First Street of the Mines*. And every street had the same old and brand-new notice: 1st Street of the Magnolia: 4th Street of Enriquez Gonzalez: very fine!

But the First Street of the Mines was just a track between the stiff living fence of organ cactus, with poinsettia trees holding up scarlet mops of flowers, and mango trees, tall and black, stonily drooping the strings of unripe fruit. The Street of the Magnolia was a rocky stream-gutter, disappearing to nowhere from nowhere, between cactus and bushes. The Street of the Vasquez was a stony stream-bed, emerging out of tall, wildly tall reeds.

Not a soul anywhere. Through the fences, half deserted gardens of trees and banana plants, each enclosure with a half-hidden hut of black adobe bricks crowned with a few old tiles for a roof, and perhaps a new wing made of twigs. Everything hidden, secret, silent. A sense of darkness among the silent mango trees, a sense of lurking, of unwillingness. Then actually some half-bold curs barking at us across the stile of one garden, a forked bough over which one must step to enter the chicken-bitten enclosure. And actually a man crossing the proudly labelled: Fifth Street of the Independence.

If there were no churches to mark a point in these villages, there would be nowhere at all to make for. The sense of nowhere is intense, between the dumb and repellent living fence of cactus. But the Spaniards, in the midst of these black, mud-brick huts, have inevitably reared the white twin-towered magnificence of a big and lonely, hopeless church; and where there is a church there will be a *plaza*. And a *plaza* is a *zócalo*, a hub. Even though the wheel does not go round, a hub is still a hub. Like the old Forum.

So we stray diffidently on, in the maze of streets which are only straight tracks between cactuses, till we see Reforma, and at the end of *Reforma*, the great church.

In front of the church is a rocky *plaza* leaking with grass, with water rushing into two big, oblong stone basins. The great church stands rather ragged, in a dense forlornness, for all the world like some big white human being, in rags, held captive in a world of ants.

On the uphill side of the *plaza*, a long low white building with a shed in front, and under the shed crowding, all the short-statured men of the *pueblo*, in their white cotton clothes and big hats. They are listening to something: but the silence is heavy, furtive, secretive. They stir like white-clad insects.

Rosalino looks sideways at them, and sheers away. Even we lower our voices to ask what is going on. Rosalino replies, *sotto voce*, that they are making *asuntos*. But what business? we insist. The dark faces of the little men under the big hats look round at us suspiciously, like dark gaps in the atmosphere. Our alien presence in this vacuous village, is like the sound of a drum in a churchyard. Rosalino mumbles unintelligibly. We stray across the forlorn yard into the church.

Thursday was the day of the Virgin of the Soledad, so the church is littered with flowers, sprays of wild yellow flowers trailing on the floor. There is a great Gulliver's Travels fresco picture of an angel having a joy-ride on the back of a Goliath. On the left, near the altar steps, is seated a life-size Christ--undersized; seated upon a little table, wearing a pair of woman's frilled knickers, a little mantle of purple silk dangling from His back, and His face bent forward gazing fatuously at His naked knee, which emerges from the needlework frill of the drawers. Across from Him a living woman is half-hidden behind a buttress, mending something, sewing.

We sit silent, motionless, in the whitewashed church ornamented with royal blue and bits of gilt. A barefoot Indian with a high-domed head comes in and kneels with his legs close together, his back stiff, at once very humble and resistant. His cotton jacket and trousers are long-unwashed rag, the colour of dry earth, and torn, so that one sees smooth pieces of brown thigh, and brown back. He kneels in a sort of intense fervour for a minute, then gets up and childishly, almost idiotically, begins to take the pieces of candle from the candlesticks. He is the Verger.

Outside, the gang of men is still pressing under the shed. We insist on knowing what is going on. Rosalino, looking sideways at them, plucks up courage to say plainly that the two men at the table are canvassing for votes: for the Government, for the State, for a new governor, whatever it may be. Votes! Votes! Votes! The farce of it! Already on the wall of the low building, on which one sees, in blue letters, the word *Justizia*, there are pasted the late political posters, with the loud announcement: Vote For This Mark (+). Or another: Vote For This Mark (-).

My dear fellow, this is when democracy becomes real fun. You vote for one red ring inside another red ring and you get a Julio Echegaray. You vote for a blue dot inside a blue ring, and you get a Socrate Ezequiel Tos. Heaven knows what you get for the two little red circles on top of one another Suppose we vote, and try. There's all sorts in the lucky bag. There might come a name like Peregrino Zenon Cocotilla.

Independence I Government by the People, of the People, for the People! We all live in the Calle de la Reforma, in Mexico.

On the bottom of the *plaza* is a shop. We want some fruit. '*Hay frutas?* Oranges or bananas?'--'*No, Señor.*'--'No fruits?'--'*No hay!*'--'Can I buy a cup?'--'*No hay.*'--'Can I buy a *jicara*, a gourd-shell that we might drink from?' '*No hay.*'.

No hay means *there isn't any*, and it's the most regular sound made by the dumb-bells of the land.

'What is there, then?' A sickly grin. There are, as a matter of fact, candles, soap, dead and withered chiles, a few dried grasshoppers, dust, and stark, bare wooden pigeon-holes. Nothing, nothing, nothing. Next-door is another little hole of a shop. *Hay frutas?--No hay.--Qué hay?--Hay tepache!*

'*Para borracharse,*' says Rosalino, with a great grin.

Tepache is a fermented drink of pineapple rinds and brown sugar: to get drunk on, as Rosalino says. But mildly drunk. There is probably *mescal* too, to get brutally drunk on.

The village is exhausted in resource. But we insist on fruit. Where, *where* can I buy oranges and bananas? I see oranges on the trees, I see banana plants.

'Up there!' The woman waves with her hand as if she were cutting the air upwards.

'That way?'

'Yes.'

We go up the Street of Independence. They have got rid of us from the *plaza*.

Another black hut with a yard, and orange-trees beyond.

'*Hay frutas?*

'*No hay.*'

'Not an orange, nor a banana?'

'*No hay.*'

We go on. *She* has got rid of us. We descend the black rocky steps to the stream, and up the other side, past the high reeds. There is a yard with heaps of maize in a shed, and tethered bullocks: and a bare-bosom, black-browed girl.

'*Hay frutas?*'

'*No hay.*'

'But Yes I There are oranges--there!'

She turns and looks at the oranges on the trees at the back, and imbecilely answers:

'*No hay.*'

It is a choice between killing her and hurrying away.

We hear a drum and a whistle. It is down a rocky black track that calls itself The Street of Benito Juarez: the same old gent who stands for all this obvious Reform, and Vote for (o).

A yard with shade round. Women kneading the maize dough, *masa*, for *tortillas*. A man lounging. And a little boy beating a kettledrum sideways, and a big man playing a little reedy wooden whistle, rapidly, endlessly, disguising the tune of *La Cucuracha*. They won't play a tune unless they can render it almost unrecognizable.

'*Hay frutas?*'

'*No hay.*'

'Then what is happening here?'

A sheepish look, and no answer.

'Why are you playing music?'

'It is a *fiesta.*'

My God, a feast! That weary *masa*, a millstone in the belly. And for the rest, the blank, heavy, dark-grey barrenness, like an adobe brick. The drum-boy rolls his big Indian eyes at us, and beats on, though filled with consternation. The flute man glances, is half appalled and half resentful, so he blows harder.

The lounging man comes and mutters to Rosalino, and Rosalino mutters back, four words.

Four words in the *idioma*, the Zapotec language. We retire, pushed silently away.

'What language do they speak here, Rosalino?'

'*The idioma.*'

'You understand them? It is Zapoteca, same as your language?'

'Yes, *Señor.*'

'Then why do you always speak in Spanish to them?'

'Because they don't speak the *idioma* of my village.'

He means, presumably, that there are dialect differences. Anyhow, he asserts his bit of Spanish, and says *Hay frutas?*

It was like a *posada*. It was like the Holy Virgin on Christmas Eve, wandering from door to door looking for a lodging in which to bear her child: Is there a room here? *No hay!*

The same with us. *Hay frutas? No hay!* We went down every straight ant-run of that blessed village. But at last we pinned a good-natured woman. 'Now tell us, *where* can we buy oranges? We see them on the trees. We want them to eat.

'Go,' she said, to Valentino Ruiz. He has oranges. Yes, he has oranges, and he sells them.' And she cut the air upwards with her hand.

From black hut to black hut went we, till at last we got to the house of Valentino Ruiz. And to I it was the yard with the *fiesta*. The lounging man was peeping out of the gateless gateway, as we came, at us.

It is the same place!' cried Rosalino, with a laugh of bashful agony.

But we don't belong to the ruling race for nothing. Into the yard we march.

'Is this the house of Valentino Ruiz? *Hay naranjas?* Are there oranges?'

We had wandered so long, and asked so often, that the *masa* was made into *tortillas*, the *tortillas* were baked, and a group of people were sitting in a ring on the ground, eating them. It was the *fiesta*.

At my question up jumped a youngish man, and a woman as if they had been sitting on a scorpion each.

'Oh, *Señor*,' said the woman, there are few oranges, and they are not ripe, as the *Señor* would want them. But pass this way.'

We pass up to the garden, past the pink roses, to a little orange-tree, with a few yellowish-green oranges.

You see; they are not ripe as you will want them,' says the youngish man.

'They will do.' Tropical oranges are always green. These, we found later, were almost insipidly sweet.

Even then, I can only get three of the big, thick-skinned, greenish oranges. But I spy sweet limes, and insist on having five or six of these.

He charges me three cents apiece for the oranges: the market price is two for five cents: and one cent each for the *limas*.

'In my village,' mutters Rosalino when we get away, 'oranges are five for one cent.'

Never mind! It is one o'clock. Let us get out of the village, where the water will be safe, and eat lunch.

In the *plaza*, the men are just dispersing, one gang coming down the hill. They watch us as if we were a coyote, a *zopilote*, and a white she-bear walking together in the street.

'*Adios!*

'*Adios!* comes the low roll of reply, like a roll of cannon shot.

The water rushes downhill in a stone gutter beside the road. We climb up the hill, up the Street of the Camomile, alongside the rushing water. At one point it crosses the road unchannelled, and we wade through it. It is the village drinking supply.

At the juncture of the roads, where the water crosses, another silent white gang of men. Again: *Adios!* and again the low, musical, deep volley of *Adios!*

Up, up wearily. We must get above the village to be able to drink the water without developing typhoid.

At last, the last house, the naked hills. We follow the water across a dry maize-field, then up along a bank. Below is a quite deep gully. Across is an orchard, and some women with baskets of fruit.

'*Hay frutas?*' calls Rosalino, in a half-voice. He is getting bold.

'*Hay,*' says an old woman, in the curious half-voice. 'But not ripe.'

Shall we go clown into the gully into the shade? No; someone is bathing among the reeds below, and the aqueduct water rushes along in the gutter here above. On, on, till we spy a wild guava tree over the channel of water. At last we can sit down and eat and drink, on a bank of dry grass, under the wild guava tree.

We put the bottle of lemonade in the aqueduct to cool. I scoop out a big half-orange, the thick rind of which makes a cup.

'Look, Rosalino! The cup!'

'*La taza!*' he cries, soft-tongued, with a bark of laughter and delight.

And one drinks the soft, rather lifeless, warmish Mexican water. But it is pure.

Over the brink of the water-channel is the gully, and a noise--chock, chock! I go to look. It is a woman, naked to the hips, standing washing her other garments upon a stone. She has a beautiful full back, of a deep orange colour, and her wet hair is divided and piled. In the water a few yards up-stream two men are sitting naked, their brown-orange giving off a glow in the shadow, also washing their clothes. Their wet hair seems to steam blue-blackness. Just above them is a sort of bridge, where the water divides, the channel-water taken from the little river, and led along the top of the bank.

We sit under the wild guava tree in silence, and eat. The old woman of the fruit, with naked breast and coffee-brown naked arms, her under-garment fastened on one shoulder, round her waist an old striped *sarape* for a skirt, and on her head a blue *rebozo* piled against the sun, comes marching down the aqueduct with black bare feet, holding three or four *chirimoyas* to her bosom. *Chirimoyas* are green custard-apples.

She lectures us, in slow, heavy Spanish:

'This water, here, is for drinking. The other, below, is for washing. This, you drink, and you don't wash in it. The other, you wash in, and you don't drink it.' And she looked inquisitively at the bottle of lemonade, cooling.

'Very good. We understand.'

Then she gave us the *chirimoyas*. I asked her to change the *peso*: I had no change.

'No, *Señor*,' she said. 'No, *Señor*. You don't pay me. I bring you these, and may you eat well. But the *chirimoyas* are not ripe: in two or three days they will be ripe. Now, they are not. In two or three days they will be. Now, they are not.

You can't eat them yet. But I make a gift of them to you, and may you eat well. Farewell. Remain with God.'

She marched impatiently off along the aqueduct.

Rosalino waited to catch my eye. Then he opened his mouth and showed his pink tongue and swelled out his throat like a cobra, in a silent laugh after the old woman.

'But,' he said in a low tone, 'the *chirimoyas* are not good ones.'

And again he swelled in the silent, delighted, derisive laugh.

He was right. When we carne to eat them, three days later, the custard-apples all had worms in them, and hardly any white meat.

'The old woman of Huayapa,' said Rosalino, reminiscent.

However, she had got her bottle. When we had drunk the lemonade, we sent Rosalino to give her the empty wine-bottle, and she made him another sententious little speech. But to her the bottle was a treasure.

And I, going round the little hummock behind the wild guava tree to throw away the papers of the picnic, came upon a golden-brown young man with his shirt just coming down over his head, but over no more of him. Hastily retreating, I thought again what beautiful, suave, rich skins these people have; a sort of richness of the flesh. It goes, perhaps, with the complete absence of what we call 'spirit'.

We lay still for a time, looking at the tiny guavas and the perfect, soft, high blue sky overhead, where the hawks and the ragged-winged *zopilotes* sway and diminish. A long, hot way home. But *mañana es otro dia*. Tomorrow is another day. And even the next five minutes are far enough away, in Mexico, on a Sunday afternoon.

3 - THE MOZO

Rosalino really goes with the house, though he has been in service here only two months. When we went to look at the place, we saw him lurking in the *patio*, and glancing furtively under his brows. He is not one of the erect, bantam little Indians that stare with a black, incomprehensible, but somewhat defiant stare. It may be Rosalino has a distant strain of other Indian blood, not Zapotec. Or it may be he is only a bit different. The difference lies in a certain sensitiveness and aloneness, as if he were a mother's boy. The way he drops his head and looks sideways under his black lashes, apprehensive, apprehending, feeling his way, as it were. Not the bold male glare of most of the Indians, who seem as if they had never, never had mothers at all.

The Aztec gods and goddesses are, as far as we have known anything about them, an unlovely and unlovable lot. In their myths there is no grace or charm, no poetry. Only this perpetual grudge, grudge, grudging, one god grudging another, the gods grudging men their existence, and men grudging the animals. The goddess of love is a goddess of dirt and prostitution, a dirt-eater, a horror, without a touch of tenderness. If the god wants to make love to her, she has to sprawl down in front of him, blatant and accessible.

And then, after all, when she conceives and brings forth, what is it she produces? What is the infant-god she tenderly bears? Guess, all ye people, joyful and triumphant!

You never could.

It is a stone knife.

It is a razor-edged knife of blackish-green flint, the knife of all knives, the veritable Paraclete of knives. It is the sacrificial knife with which the priest makes a gash in his victim's breast, before he tears out the heart, to hold it smoking to the sun.

And the Sun, the Sun behind the sun, is supposed to suck the smoking heart greedily with insatiable appetite.

This, then, is a pretty Christmas Eve. Lo, the goddess is gone to bed, to bring forth her child. Lo! ye people, await the birth of the saviour, the wife of a god is about to become a mother.

Tarumm-tarah! Tarumm-tarah! blow the trumpets. The child is born. Unto us a son is given. Bring him forth, lay him on a tender cushion. Show him, then, to all the people. See! See! See him upon the cushion, tenderly new-born and reposing! Ah, *qué bonito!* Oh, what a nice, blackish, smooth, keen stone knife!

And to this day, most of the Mexican Indian women seem to bring forth stone knives. Look at them, these sons of incomprehensible mothers, with their black eyes like flints, and their stiff little bodies as taut and as keen as knives of obsidian. Take care they don't rip you up.

Our Rosalino is an exception. He drops his shoulders just a little. He is a bit bigger, also, than the average Indian down here. He must be about five feet four inches. And he hasn't got the big, obsidian, glaring eyes. His eyes are smaller, blacker, like the quick black eyes of the lizard. They don't look at one with the obsidian stare. They are just a bit aware that there is another being, unknown, at the other end of the glance. Hence he drops his head with a little apprehension, screening himself as if he were vulnerable.

Usually, these people have no correspondence with one at all. To them a white man or white woman is a sort of phenomenon; just as a monkey is a sort of phenomenon; something to watch, and wonder at, and laugh at, but not to be taken on one's own plane.

Now the white man is a sort of extraordinary white monkey that, by cunning, has learnt lots of semi-magical secrets of the universe, and made himself boss of the show. Imagine a race of big white monkeys got up in fantastic clothes, and able to kill a man by hissing at him; able to leap through the air in great hops, covering a mile in each leap; able to transmit his thoughts by a moment's effort of concentration to some great white monkey or monkeyess, a thousand miles away: and you have, from our point of view, something of the picture that the Indian has of us.

The white monkey has curious tricks. He knows, for example, the time. Now to a Mexican, and an Indian, time is a vague, foggy reality. There are only three times: *en la mañana, en la tarde, en la troche*, in the morning, in the afternoon, in the night. There is even no midday, and no evening.

But to the white monkey, horrible to relate, there are exact spots of time, such as five o'clock, half past nine. The day is a horrible puzzle of exact spots of time.

The same with distance: horrible invisible distances called two miles, ten miles. To the Indians, there is near and far, and very near and very far. There is two days or one day. But two miles are as good as twenty to him, for he goes entirely by his feeling. If a certain two miles feels far to him, then it *is* far, it is *muy lejos*! But if a certain twenty miles *feels* near and familiar, then it is not far. Oh, no, it is just a little distance. And he will let you set off in the evening, for night to overtake you in the wilderness, without a qualm. It is not far.

But the white man has a horrible, truly horrible, monkey-like passion for invisible exactitudes. *Mañana*, to the native, may mean tomorrow, three days hence, six months hence, and never. There are no fixed points in life, save birth, and death, and the *fiestas*. The fixed points of birth and death evaporate spontaneously into vagueness. And the priests fix the *fiestas*. From time immemorial priests have fixed the *fiestas*, the festivals of the gods, and men have had no more to do with time. What should men have to do with time?

The same with money. These *centavos* and these *pesos*, what do they mean, after all? Little discs that have no charm. The natives insist on reckoning in invisible coins, coins that don't exist here, like *reales* or *pesetas*. If you buy two eggs for a *real*, you have to pay twelve and a half *centavos*. Since also half a *centavo* doesn't exist, you or the vendor forfeit the non-existent.

The same with honesty, the *meum* and the *tuum*. The white man has a horrible way of remembering, even to a *centavo*, even to a thimbleful of *mescal*. Horrible! The Indian, it seems to me, is not naturally dishonest. He is not naturally avaricious, has not even any innate cupidity. In this he is unlike the old people of the Mediterranean, to whom possessions have a mystic meaning, and a silver coin a mystic white halo, a *lueur* of magic.

To the real Mexican, no! He doesn't care. He doesn't even *like* keeping money. His deep instinct is to spend it at once, so that he needn't have it. He doesn't really want to keep anything, not even his wife and children. Nothing that he has to be responsible for. Strip, strip, strip away the past and the future, leave the naked moment of the present disentangled. Strip away memory, strip away forethought and care; leave the moment, stark and sharp and without consciousness, like the obsidian knife. The before and the after are the stuff of consciousness. The instant moment is for ever keen with a razor-edge of oblivion, like the knife of sacrifice.

But the great white monkey has got hold of the keys of the world, and the black-eyed Mexican has to serve the great white monkey, in order to live. He has to learn the tricks of the white monkey-show: time of the day, coin of money, machines that start at a second, work that is meaningless and yet is paid for with exactitude, in exact coin. A whole existence of monkey-tricks and monkey-virtues. The strange monkey-virtue of charity, the white monkeys nosing round to *help*, to *save!* Could any trick be more unnatural? Yet it is one of the tricks of the great white monkey.

If an Indian is poor, he says to another: I have no food; give me to eat. Then the other hands the hungry one a couple of *tortillas*. That is natural. But when the white monkey comes round, they peer at the house, at the woman, at the children. They say: Your child is sick. *Si, Señor.* What have you done for it-- *Nothing. What is to be done?*--You must make a poultice. I will show you how.

Well, it was very amusing, this making hot dough to dab on the baby. Like plastering a house with mud. But why do it twice? Twice is not amusing. The child will die. Well, then, it will be in Paradise. How nice for it! That's just what God wants of it, that it shall be a cheerful little angel among the roses of Paradise. What could be better?

How tedious of the white monkey coming with the trick of salvation, to rub oil on the baby, and put poultices on it, and make you give it medicine in a spoon at morning, noon, and night. Why morning and noon and night? Why not just anytime, anywhen? It will die tomorrow if you don't do these things today! But tomorrow is another day, and it is not dead now, so if it dies at another time, it must be because the other times are out of hand.

Oh, the tedious, exacting white monkeys, with their yesterdays and todays and tomorrows! Tomorrow is always another day, and yesterday is part of the encircling never. Why think outside the moment? And inside the moment one does not think. So why pretend to think? It is one of the white-monkey-tricks. He is a clever monkey. But he is ugly, and he has nasty, white flesh. We are not ugly, with screwed-up faces, and we have good warm-brown flesh. If we have to work for the white monkey, we don't care. His tricks are half-amusing. And one may as well amuse oneself that way as any other. So long as one is amused.

So long as the devil does not rouse in us, seeing the white monkeys for ever mechanically bossing, with their incessant tick-tack of work. Seeing them get the work out of us, the sweat, the money, and then taking the very land from us, the very oil and metal out of our soil.

They do it! They do it all the time. Because they can't help it. Because grasshoppers can but hop, and ants can carry little sticks, and white monkeys can go tick-tack, tick-tack, do this, do that, time to work, time to eat, time to drink, time to sleep, time to walk, time to ride, time to wash, time to look dirty, tick-tack, tick-tack, time, time, time! time! Oh, cut off his nose and make him swallow it.

For the *moment* is as changeless as an obsidian knife, and the heart of the Indian is keen as the moment that divides past from future, and sacrifices them both.

To Rosalino, too, the white monkey-tricks are amusing. He is ready to work for the white monkeys, to learn some of their tricks, their monkey-speech of Spanish, their tick-tack ways. He works for four *pesos* a month, and his food: a few *tortillas*. Four *pesos* are two American dollars: about nine shillings. He owns two cotton shirts, two pairs of calico pantaloons, two blouses, one of pink cotton, one of darkish flannelette, and a pair of sandals. Also, his straw hat that he has curled up to look very jaunty, and a rather old, factory-made, rather cheap shawl, or plaid rug with fringe. *Et praeterea nihil.*

His duty is to rise in the morning and sweep the street in front of the house, and water it. Then he sweeps and waters the broad, brick-tiled verandas, and flicks the chairs with a sort of duster made of fluffy reeds. After which he walks behind the cook--she is very superior, had a Spanish grandfather, and Rosalino must address her as *Señora*--carrying the basket to market. Returned from the market, he sweeps the whole of the *patio*, gathers up the leaves and refuse, fills the pannier-basket, hitches it up on to his shoulders, and holds it by a band across his forehead, and thus, a beast of burden, goes out to deposit the garbage at the side of one of the little roads leading out of the city. Every little road leaves the town between heaps of garbage, an avenue of garbage blistering in the sun.

Returning, Rosalino waters the whole of the garden and sprinkles the whole of the *patio*. This takes most of the morning. In the afternoon, he sits without much to do. If the wind has blown or the day is hot, he starts again at about three o'clock, sweeping up leaves, and sprinkling everywhere with an old watering-can.

Then he retreats to the entrance-way, the *zaguán*, which, with its big doors and its cobbled track, is big enough to admit an ox-wagon. The *zaguán* is his home: just the doorway. In one corner is a low wooden bench about four feet long and eighteen inches wide. On this he screws up and sleeps, in his clothes as he is, wrapped in the old *sarape*.

But this is anticipating. In the obscurity of the *zaguán* he sits and pores, pores, pores over a school-book, learning to read and write. He can read a bit, and write a bit. He filled a large sheet of foolscap with writing: quite nice. But I found out that what he had written was a Spanish poem, a love-poem, with *no puedo olvidar* and *voy a cortar*--the rose, of course. He had written the thing straight ahead, without verse-lines or capitals or punctuation at all, just a vast string of words, a whole foolscap sheet full. When I read a few lines aloud, he writhed and laughed in an agony of confused feelings. And of what he had written he understood a small, small amount, parrot-wise, from the top of his head. Actually, it meant just words, sound, noise, to him: noise called *Castellano*, Castilian. Exactly like a parrot.

From seven to eight he goes to the night-school, to cover a bit more of the foolscap. He has been going for two years. If he goes two years more he will perhaps really be able to read and write six intelligible sentences: but only Spanish, which is as foreign to him as Hindustani would be to an English farm-boy. Then if he can speak his quantum of Spanish, and read it and write it to a very uncertain extent, he will return to his village two days' journey on foot into the hills, and then, in time, he may even rise to be an *alcalde*, or headman of the village, responsible to the Government. If he were *alcalde* he would get a little salary. But far more important to him is the glory: being able to boss.

He has a *paisano*, a fellow-countryman, to sleep with him in the *zaguán*, to guard the doors. Whoever gets into the house or *patio* must get through these big doors. There is no other entrance, not even a needle's eye. The windows to the street are heavily barred. Each house is its own small fortress. Ours is a double square, the trees and flowers in the first square, with the two wings of the house. And in the second *patio*, the chickens, pigeons, guinea-pigs, and the big heavy earthenware dish or tub, called an *apaxtle*, in which all the servants can bathe themselves, like chickens in a saucer.

By half past nine at night Rosalino is lying on his little bench, screwed up, wrapped in his shawl, his sandals, called *huaraches*, on the floor. Usually he takes off his *huaraches* when he goes to bed. That is all his preparation. In another corner, wrapped up, head and all, like a mummy in his thin old blanket, the *paisano*, another lad of about twenty, lies asleep on the cold stones. And at an altitude of five thousand feet, the nights can be cold.

Usually everybody is in by half past nine in our very quiet house. If not, you may thunder at the big doors. It is hard to wake Rosalino. You have to go close to him, and call. That will wake him. But don't touch him. That would startle him terribly. No one is touched unawares, except to be robbed or murdered.

'Rosalino! *están tocando*!'--'Rosalino! they are knocking!'

At last there starts up a strange, glaring, utterly lost Rosa-lino. Perhaps he just has enough wit to pull the door-catch. One wonders where he was, and what he was, in his sleep, he starts up so strange and wild and lost.

The first time he had anything to do for me was when the van was come to carry the bit of furniture to the house. There was Aurelio, the dwarf *mozo* of our friends and Rosalino, and the man who drove the wagon. But there *should* have been also a *cargador*--a porter. 'Help them,' said I to Rosalino.

'You give a hand to help.' But he winced away, muttering, '*No quiero*!--I don't want to.'

The fellow, I thought to myself, is a fool. He thinks it's not his job, and perhaps he is afraid of smashing the furniture. Nothing to be done but to leave him alone.

We settled in, and Rosalino seemed to like doing things for us. He liked learning his monkey-tricks from the white monkeys. And since we started feeding him from our own meals, and for the first time in his life he had real soups, meat-stews, or a fried egg, he loved to do things in the kitchen. He would come with sparkling black eyes: '*Hé comido el caldo. Grazias*!' (I have eaten the soup. Thank you.')--And he would give a strange, excited little yelp of a laugh.

Came the day when we walked to Huayapa, on the Sunday, and he was very thrilled. But at night, in the evening when we got home, he lay mute on his bench--not that he was really tired. The Indian gloom, which settles on them like a black marsh-fog, had settled on him. He did not bring in the water--let me carry it by myself.

Monday morning, the same black, reptilian gloom, and a sense of hatred. He hated us. This was a bit flabbergasting, because he had been so thrilled and happy the day before. But the revulsion had come. He didn't forgive himself for having felt free and happy with us. He had eaten what we had eaten, hard-boiled eggs and sardine sandwiches and cheese; he had drunk out of the orange-peel *taza*, which delighted him so much. He had had a bottle of *gaseosa*, fizz, with us, on the way home, in San Felipe.

And now, the reaction. The flint knife. He had been happy, *therefore* we were scheming to take another advantage of him. We had some devilish white monkey-trick up our sleeve; we wanted to get at his *soul*, no doubt, and do it the white monkey's damage. We wanted to get at his heart, did we? But his heart was an obsidian knife.

He hated us, and gave off a black steam of hate, that filled the *patio* and made one feel sick. He did not come to the kitchen, he did not carry the water. Leave him alone.

At lunch-time on Monday he said he wanted to leave. Why? He said he wanted to go back to his village.

Very well. He was to wait just a few days, till another *mozo* was found.

At this a glance of pure, reptilian hate from his black eyes.

He sat motionless on his bench all the afternoon, in the Indian stupor of gloom and profound hate. In the evening, he cheered up a little and said he would stay on, at least till Easter.

Tuesday morning. More stupor and gloom and hate. He wanted to go back to his village at once. All right! No one wanted to keep him against his will. Another *mozo* would be found at once.

He went off in the numb stupor of gloom and hate, a very potent hate that could affect one in the pit of one's stomach with nausea.

Tuesday afternoon, and he thought he would stay.

Wednesday morning, and he wanted to go.

Very good. Inquiries made; another *mozo* was coming on Friday morning. It was settled.

Thursday was *fiesta*. Wednesday, therefore, we would go to market, the Nina-- that is the mistress--myself, and Rosalino with the basket. He loved to go to market with the *patrones*. We would give him money and send him off to bargain for oranges, *pitahayas*, potatoes, eggs, a chicken, and so forth. This he simply loved to do. It put him into a temper to see us buying without bargaining, and paying ghastly prices.

He bargained away, silent almost, muttering darkly. It took him a long time, but he had far greater success than even Natividad, the cook. And he came back in triumph, with much stuff and little money spent.

So again that afternoon, he was staying on. The spell was wearing off.

The Indians of the hills have a heavy, intense sort of attachment to their villages; Rosalino had not been out of the little city for two years. Suddenly finding himself in Huayapa, a real Indian hill-village, the black Indian gloom of nostalgia must have made a crack in his spirits. But he had been perfectly cheerful--perhaps too cheerful--till we got home.

Again, the Señorita had taken a photograph of him. They are all crazy to have their photographs taken. I had given him an envelope and a stamp, to send a photograph to his mother. Because in his village he had a widow mother, a brother, and a married sister. The family owned a bit of land, with orange-trees. The best oranges come from the hills, where it is cooler. Seeing the photographs, the mother, who had completely forgotten her son, as far as any keen remembering goes, suddenly, like a cracker going off inside her, wanted him: at that very moment. So she sent an urgent message.

But already it was Wednesday afternoon. Arrived a little fellow in white clothes, smiling hard. It was the brother from the hills. Now, we thought, Rosalino will have someone to walk back with. On Friday, after the *fiesta*, he would go.

Thursday, he escorted us with the basket to the *fiesta*. He bargained for flowers, and for a *sarape* which he didn't get, for a carved *jicara* which he did get, and for a number of toys. He and the Nina and the Señorita ate a great wafer of a pancake with sweet stuff on it. The basket grew heavy. The brother appeared, to carry the hen and the extra things. Bliss.

He was perfectly happy again. He didn't want to go on Friday; he didn't want to go at all. He wanted to stay with us and come with us to England when we went home.

So, another trip to the friend, the Mexican, who had found us the other *mozo*. Now to put off the other boy again: but then, they are like that.

And the Mexican, who had known Rosalino when he first carne down from the hills and could speak no Spanish, told us another thing about him.

In the last revolution--a year ago--the revolutionaries of the winning side wanted more soldiers from the hills. The *alcalde* of the hill-village was told to pick out young men and send them down to the barracks in the city. Rosalino was among the chosen.

But Rosalino refused, said again No *quiero*! He is one of those, like myself, who have a horror of serving in a mass of men, or even f being mixed up with a mass of men. He obstinately refused, Whereupon the recruiting soldiers heat him with the butts of their rifles till he lay unconscious, apparently dead.

Then, because they wanted him at once, and he would now be no good for some time, with his injured back, they left him, to get the revolution over without him.

This explains his fear of furniture-carrying, and his fear of being 'caught'.

Yet that little Aurelio, the friend's *mozo*, who is not above four feet six in height, a tiny fellow, fared even worse, He, too, is from the hills. In this village, a cousin of his gave some information to the *losing* side in the revolution. The cousin wisely disappeared.

But in the city, the winning side seized Aurelio, since he was the *cousin* of the delinquent. In spite of the fact that he was the faithful *mozo* of a foreign resident, he was flung into prison. Prisoners in prison are not fed. Either friends or relatives bring them food, or they go very, very thin. Aurelio had a married sister in town, but *she* was afraid to go to the prison lest she and her husband should be seized. The master, then, sent his new *mozo* twice a day to the prison with a basket; the huge, huge prison, for this little town of a few thousands.

Meanwhile the master struggled and struggled with the 'authorities'--friends of the people--for Aurelio's release. Nothing to be done.

One day the new *mozo* arrived at the prison with the basket, to find no Aurelio. A friendly soldier gave the message Aurelio had left. '*Adios a mi patrón. Me llevan.*' Oh, fatal words: '*Me llevan.*'--They are taking me off. The master rushed to the train: it had gone, with the dwarf, plucky little *mozo*, into the void.

Months later, Aurelio reappeared. He was in rags, haggard, and his dark throat was swollen up to the ears. He had been taken off, two hundred miles into Vera Cruz State. He had been hung up by the neck, with a fixed knot, and left hanging for hours. Why? To make the cousin come and save his relative: put his own neck into a running noose. To make the absolutely innocent fellow confess: what? Everybody knew he was innocent. At any rate, to teach everybody better next time. Oh, brotherly teaching!

Aurelio escaped, and took to the mountains. Sturdy little dwarf of a fellow, he made his way back, begging *tortillas* at the villages, and arrived, haggard, with a great swollen neck, to find his master waiting, and another 'party' in power. More friends of the people.

Tomorrow is another day. The master nursed Aurelio well, and Aurelio is a strong, if tiny, fellow, with big, brilliant black eyes that for the moment will trust a foreigner, but none of his own people. A dwarf in stature, but perfectly made, and very strong. And very intelligent, far more quick and intelligent than Rosalino.

Is it any wonder that Aurelio and Rosalino, when they see the soldiers with guns on their shoulders marching towards the prison with some blanched prisoner between them--and one sees it every few days--stand and gaze in a blank kind of horror, and look at the *patrón*, to see if there is any refuge?

Not to be *caught!* Not to be *caught!* It must have been the prevailing motive of Indian-Mexico life since long before Montezuma marched his prisoners to sacrifice.

4 - MARKET DAY

This is the last Saturday before Christmas. The next year will be momentous, one feels. This year is nearly gone. Dawn was windy, shaking the leaves, and the rising sun shone under a gap of yellow cloud. But at once it touched the yellow flowers that rise above the *patio* wall, and the swaying, glowing magenta of the bougainvillea, and the fierce red outbursts of the poinsettia. The poinsettia is very splendid, the flowers very big, and of a sure stainless red. They call them Noche Buenas, flowers of Christmas Eve. These tufts throw out their scarlet sharply, like red birds ruffling in the wind of dawn as if going to bathe, all their feathers alert. This for Christmas, instead of holly-berries. Christmas seems to need a red herald.

The yucca is tall, higher than the house. It is, too, in flower, hanging an arm's-length of soft creamy bells, like a yard-long grape-cluster of foam. And the waxy bells break on their stems in the wind, fall noiselessly from the long creamy bunch, that hardly sways.

The coffee-berries are turning red. The hibiscus flowers, rose-coloured, sway at the tips of the thin branches, in rosettes of soft red.

In the second *patio*, there is a tall tree of the flimsy acacia sort. Above itself it puts up whitish fingers of flowers, naked on the blue sky. And in the wind these fingers of flowers in the bare blue sky, sway, sway with the reeling, roundward motion of tree-tips in a wind.

A restless morning, with clouds lower down, moving also with a larger roundward motion. Everything moving. Best to go out in motion too, the slow roundward motion like the hawks.

Everything seems slowly to circle and hover towards a central point, the clouds, the mountains round the valley, the dust that rises, the big, beautiful, white-barred hawks, *gabilanes*, and even the snow-white flakes of flowers upon the dim *palo-blanco* tree. Even the organ cactus, rising in stock-straight clumps, and the candelabrum cactus, seem to be slowly wheeling and pivoting upon a centre, close upon it.

Strange that we should think in straight lines, when there are none, and talk of straight courses, when every course, sooner or later, is seen to be making the sweep round, swooping upon the centre. When space is curved, and the cosmos is sphere within sphere, and the way from any point to any other point is round the bend of the inevitable, that turns as the tips of the broad wings of the hawk turn upwards, leaning upon the air like the invisible half of the ellipse. If I have a way to go, it will be round the swoop of a bend impinging centripetal towards the centre. The straight course is hacked out in wounds, against the will of the world.

Yet the dust advances like a ghost along the road, down the valley plain. The dry turf of the valley-bed gleams like soft skin, sunlit and pinkish ochre, spreading wide between the mountains that seem to emit their own darkness, a dark-blue vapour translucent, sombring them from the humped crests downwards. The many-pleated, noiseless mountains of Mexico.

And away on the footslope lie the white specks of Huayapa, among its lake of trees. It is Saturday, and the white dots of men are threading down the trail over the bare humps to the plain, following the dark twinkle-movement of asses, the dark nodding of the woman's head as she rides between the baskets. Saturday and market-day, and morning, so the white specks of men, like sea-gulls on plough-land, come ebbing like sparks from the *palo-blanco*, over the fawn undulating of the valley slope.

They are dressed in snow-white cotton, and they lift their knees in the Indian trot, following the ass where the woman sits perched between the huge baskets, her child tight in the *rebozo*, at the brown breast. And girls in long, full, soiled cotton skirts running, trotting, ebbing along after the twinkle-movement of the ass. Down they come in families, in clusters, in solitary ones, threading with ebbing, running, barefoot movement noiseless towards the town, that blows the bubbles of its church-domes above the stagnant green of trees, away under the opposite fawn-skin hills.

But down the valley middle comes the big road, almost straight. You will know it by the tall walking of the dust, that hastens also towards the town, overtaking, overpassing everybody. Overpassing all the dark little figures and the white specks that thread tinily, in a sort of underworld, to the town.

From the valley villages and from the mountains the peasants and the Indians are coming in with supplies, the road is like a pilgrimage, with the dust in greatest haste, dashing for town. Dark-eared asses and running men, running women, running girls, running lads, twinkling donkeys ambling on fine little feet, under twin baskets with tomatoes and gourds, twin great nets of bubble-shaped jars, twin bundles of neat-cut faggots of wood, neat as bunches of cigarettes, and twin net-sacks of charcoal. Donkeys, mules, on they come, pannier baskets making a rhythm under the perched woman, great bundles bouncing against the sides of the slim-footed animals. A baby donkey trotting naked after its piled-up dam, a white, sandal-footed man following with the silent Indian haste, and a girl running again on light feet.

Onwards, on a strange current of haste. And slowly rowing among the, foot-travel, the ox-wagons rolling solid wheels below the high net of the body. Slow oxen, with heads pressed down nosing to the earth, swaying, swaying their great horns as a snake sways itself, the shovel-shaped collar of solid wood pressing down on their necks like a scoop. On, on between the burnt-up turf and the solid, monumental green of the organ cactus. Past the rocks and the floating *palo-blanco* flowers, past the towsled dust of the mesquite bushes. While the dust once more, in a greater haste than anyone, comes tall and rapid down the road, overpowering and obscuring all the little people, as in a cataclysm.

They are mostly small people, of the Zapotec race: small men with lifted chests and quick, lifted knees, advancing with heavy energy in the midst of dust. And quiet, small, round-headed women running barefoot, tightening their blue *rebozos* round their shoulders, so often with a baby in the fold. The white cotton clothes of the men so white that their faces are invisible places of darkness under their big hats. Clothed darkness, faces of night, quickly, silently, with inexhaustible energy advancing to the town.

And many of the *serranos*, the Indians from the hills, wearing their little conical black felt hats, seem capped with night, above the straight white shoulders. Some have come far, walking all yesterday in their little black hats and black-sheathed sandals. Tomorrow they will walk .back. And their eyes will be just the same, black and bright and wild, in the dark faces. They have no goal, any more than the hawks in the air, and no course to run, any more than the clouds.

The market is a huge roofed-in place. Most extraordinary is the noise that comes out, as you pass along the adjacent street. It is a huge noise, yet you may never notice it. It sounds as if all the ghosts in the world were talking to one another, in ghost-voices, within the darkness of the market structure. It is a noise something like rain, or banana leaves in a wind. The market, full of Indians, dark-faced, silent-footed, hush-spoken, but pressing in in countless numbers. The queer hissing murmurs of the Zapotec *idioma*, among the sounds of Spanish, the quiet, aside, voices of the Mixtecas.

To buy and to sell, but above all, to commingle. In the old world, men make themselves two great excuses for coming together to a centre, and commingling freely in a mixed, unsuspicious host. Market and religion. These alone bring men, unarmed, together since time began. A little load of firewood, a woven blanket, a few eggs and tomatoes are excuse enough for men, women, and children to cross the foot-weary miles of valley and mountain. To buy, to sell, to barter, to exchange. To exchange, above all things, human contact.

That is why they like you to bargain, even if it's only the difference of a *centavo*. Round the centre of the covered market where there is a basin of water, are the flowers: red, white, pink roses in heaps, many-coloured little carnations, poppies, bits of larkspur, lemon and orange marigolds, buds of madonna lilies, pansies, a few forget-me-nots. They don't bring the tropical flowers. Only the lilies come wild from the hills, and the mauve red orchids.

'How much this bunch of cherry-pie heliotrope?' 'Fifteen *centavos*.'

'Ten.'

'Fifteen.'

You put back the cherry-pie, and depart. But the woman is quite content. The contact, so short even, brisked her up. 'Pinks?'

'The red one, Señorita? Thirty *centavos*.'

'No. I don't want red ones. The mixed.'

'Ah!' The woman seizes a handful of little carnations of all colours, carefully puts them together. 'Look, Señorita! No more?'

'No, no more. How much?'

'The same. Thirty *centavos*.'

'It is much.'

'No, Señorita, it is not much. Look at this little bunch. It is eight *centavos*.'-- Displays a scrappy little bunch. Come then, twenty-five.'

'No! Twenty-two.'

'Look!' She gathers up three or four more flowers, and claps them to the bunch. 'Two *reales*, Señorita.'

It is a bargain. Off you go with multicoloured pinks, and the woman has had one more moment of contact, with a stranger, a perfect stranger. An intermingling of voices, a threading together of different wills. It is life. The *centavos* are an excuse.

The stalls go off in straight lines, to the right, brilliant vegetables, to the left, bread and sweet buns. Away at the one end, cheese, butter, eggs, chicken, turkeys, meat. At the other, the native-woven blankets and *rebozos*, skirts, shirts, handkerchiefs. Down the far-side, sandals and leather things.

The *sarape* men spy you, and whistle to you like ferocious birds, and call 'Señor! Señor! Look!' Then with violence one flings open a dazzling blanket, while another whistles more ear-piercingly still, to make you look at *his* blanket. It is the veritable den of lions and tigers, that spot where the *sarape* men have their blankets piled on the ground. You shake your head, and flee.

To find yourself in the leather avenue.

'Señor! *Señora* Look! *Huaraches!* Very fine, very finely made! Look, Señor!'

The fat leather man jumps up and holds a pair of sandals at one's breast. They are of narrow woven strips of leather, in the newest Paris style, but a style ancient to these natives. You take them in your hand, and look at them quizzically, while the fat wife of the *huarache* man reiterates, 'Very fine work. Very fine. Much work!'

Leather men usually seem to have their wives with them. 'How much?'

'Twenty *reales*.'

'Twenty!'--in a voice of surprise and pained indignation. 'How much do you give?'

You refuse to answer. Instead you put the *huaraches* to your nose. The *huarache* man looks at his wife, and they laugh aloud.

'They smell,' you say.

'No, *Señor*, they don't smell!'--and the two go off into fits of laughter.

'Yes, they smell. It is not American leather.'

'Yes, *Señor*, it is American leather. They don't smell, *Señor*. No, they don't smell.' He coaxes you till you wouldn't believe your own nose.

'Yes, they smell.'

'How much do you give?'

'Nothing, because they smell.'

And you give another sniff, though it is painfully unnecessary. And in spite of your refusal to bid, the man and wife go into fits of laughter to see you painfully sniffing.

You lay down the sandals and shake your head.

'How much do you offer?' reiterates the man, gaily.

You shake your head mournfully, and move away. The leather man and his wife look at one another and go off into another fit of laughter, because you smelt the *huaraches*, and said they stank.

They did. The natives use human excrement for tanning leather. When Bernal Diaz came with Cortés to the great market-place of Mexico City, in Montezuma's day, he saw the little pots of human excrement in rows for sale, and the leather-makers going round sniffing to see which was the best, before they paid for it. It staggered even a fifteenth-century Spaniard. Yet my leather man and his wife think it screamingly funny that I smell the *huaraches* before buying them. Everything has its own smell, and the natural smell of *huaraches* is what it is. You might as well quarrel with an onion for smelling like an onion.

The great press of the quiet natives, some of them bright and clean, many in old rags, the brown flesh showing through the rents in the dirty cotton. Many wild hillmen, in their little hats of conical black felt, with their wild, staring eyes. And as they cluster round the hat-stall, in a long, long suspense of indecision before they can commit themselves, trying on a new hat, their black hair gleams blue-black, and falls thick and rich over their foreheads, like gleaming bluey-black feathers.

And one is reminded again of the blue-haired Buddha, with the lotus at his navel.

But already the fleas are travelling under one's clothing.

Market lasts all day. The native inns are great dreary yards with little sheds, and little rooms around. Some men and families who have come from far, will sleep in one or other of the little stall-like rooms. Many will sleep on the stones, on the earth, round the market, anywhere. But the asses are there by the hundred, crowded in the inn-yards, drooping their ears with the eternal patience of the beast that knows better than any other beast that every road curves round to the same centre of rest, and hither and thither means nothing.

And towards nightfall the dusty road will be thronged with shadowy people and unladen asses and new-laden mules, urging silently into the country again, their backs to the town, glad to get away from the town, to see the cactus and the pleated hills, and the trees that mean a village. In some village they will lie under a tree, or under a wall, and sleep. Then the next day, home.

It is fulfilled, what they came to market for. They have sold and bought. But more than that, they have had their moment of contact and centripetal flow. They have been part of a great stream of men flowing to a centre, to the vortex of the marketplace. And here they have felt life concentrate upon them, they have been jammed between the soft hot bodies of strange men come from afar, they have had the sound of strangers' voices in their ears, they have asked and been answered in unaccustomed ways.

There is no goal, and no abiding-place, and nothing is fixed, not even the cathedral towers. The cathedral towers are slowly leaning, seeking the curve of return. As the natives curved in a strong swirl, towards the vortex of the market. Then on a strong swerve of repulsion, curved out and away again, into space.

Nothing but the touch, the spark of contact. That, no more. That, which is most elusive, still the only treasure. Come, and gone, and yet the clue itself.

True, folded up in the handkerchief inside the shirt, are the copper *centavos*, and maybe a few silver *pesos*. But these too will disappear as the stars disappear at daybreak, as they are meant to disappear. Everything is meant to disappear. Every curve plunges into the vortex and is lost, re-emerges with a certain relief and takes to the open, and there is lost again.

Only that which is utterly intangible, matters. The contact, the spark of exchange. That which can never be fastened upon, for ever gone, for ever coming, never to be detained: the spark of contact.

Like the evening star, when it is neither night nor day. Like the evening star, between the sun and the moon, and swayed by neither of them. The flashing intermediary, the evening star that is seen only at the dividing of the day and night, but then is more wonderful than either.

5 - INDIANS AND ENTERTAINMENT

We go to the theatre to be entertained. It may be *The Potters*, it may be *Max Reinhardt*, *King Lear*, or *Electra*. All entertainment.

We want to be taken out of ourselves. Or not entirely that. We want to become spectators at our own show. We lean down from the plush seats like little gods in a democratic heaven, and see ourselves away below there, on the world of the stage, in a brilliant artificial sunlight, behaving comically absurdly, like Pa Potter, yet getting away with it, or behaving tragically absurdly, like King Lear, and not getting away with it: rather proud of not getting away with it.

We see ourselves: we survey ourselves: we laugh at ourselves: we weep over ourselves: we are the gods above of our own destinies. Which is very entertaining.

The secret of it all, is that we detach ourselves from the painful and always sordid trammels of actual existence, and become creatures of memory and of spirit-like consciousness. We are the gods and there's the machine, down below us. Down below, on the stage, our mechanical or earth-bound self stutters or raves, Pa Potter or King Lear. But however Potterish or Learian we may be, while we sit aloft in plush seats we are creatures of pure consciousness, pure spirit, surveying those selves of clay who are so absurd or so tragic, below.

Even a little girl trailing a long skirt and playing at being Mrs Paradiso next door, is enjoying the same sensation. From her childish little consciousness she is making Mrs Paradiso, creating her according to her own fancy. It is the little individual consciousness lording it, for the moment, over the actually tiresome and inflexible world of actuality. Mrs Paradiso in the flesh is a thing to fear. But if I can play at being Mrs Paradiso, why, then I am a little Lord Almighty, and Mrs Paradiso is but a creation from my consciousness:

The audience in the theatre is a little democracy of the ideal consciousness. They all sit there, gods of the ideal mind, and survey with laughter or tears the realm of actuality.

Which is very soothing and satisfying so long as you believe that the ideal mind is the actual arbiter. So long as you instinctively feel that there is some supreme, universal Ideal Consciousness swaying all destiny.

When you begin to have misgivings, you sit rather uneasily on your plush seat.

Nobody really believes that destiny is an accident. The very fact that day keeps on following night, and summer winter, establishes the belief in universal law, and from this to a belief in some great hidden mind in the universe is an inevitable step for us.

A few people, the so-called advanced, have grown uneasy in their bones about the Universal Mind. But the mass are absolutely convinced. And every member of the mass is absolutely convinced that he is part and parcel of this Universal Mind. Hence his joy at the theatre. His even greater joy at the cinematograph.

In the moving pictures he has detached himself even further from the solid stuff of earth. There, the people are truly shadows: the shadow-pictures are thinkings of his mind. They live in the rapid and kaleidoscopic realm of the abstract. And the individual watching the shadow-spectacle sits a very god, in an orgy of abstraction, actually dissolved into delighted, watchful spirit. And if his best girl sits beside him, she vibrates in the same ether, and triumphs in the same orgy of abstraction. No wonder this passion of dramatic abstraction becomes a lust.

That is our idea of entertainment.

You come to the Indian and ask him about his. He hasn't got one.

The Indians dance around the drum, singing. They have their great spectacular dances, Eagle dance, Corn dance. They have the dancing, singing procession between the fires at Christmas. They have their sacred races, down the long track.

White people always, or nearly always, write sentimentally about the Indians. Even a man like Adolf Bandelier. He was not a sentimental man. On the contrary. Yet the sentimentality creeps in, when he writes about the thing he knows best, the Indian.

So it is with all of them, anthropologists and myth-transcribers and all. There is that creeping note of sentimentality through it all, which makes one shrug one's shoulders and wish the Indians to hell, along with a lot of other bunk.

You've got to de-bunk the Indians, as you've got to debunk the Cowboy. When you've de-bunked the Cowboy, there's not much left. But the Indian bunk is not the Indian's invention. It is ours.

It is almost impossible for the white people to approach the Indian without either sentimentality or dislike. The common healthy vulgar white usually feels a certain native dislike of these drumming aboriginals. The highbrow invariably lapses into sentimentalism like the smell of bad eggs.

Why?--Both the reactions are due to the same feeling in the white man. The Indian is not in line with us. He's not coming our way. His whole being is going a different way from ours. And the minute you set eyes on him you know it.

And then, there's only two things you can do. You can detest the insidious devil for having an utterly different way from our own great way. Or you can perform the mental trick, and fool yourself and others into believing that the befeathered and bedaubed darling is nearer to the true ideal gods than we are.

This last is just bunk, and a lie. But it saves our appearances. The former feeling, of instinctive but tolerant repulsion, the feeling of most ordinary farmers and ranchers and mere individuals in the west, is quite natural, it is only honesty to admit it.

The Indian way of consciousness is different from and fatal to our way of consciousness. Our way of consciousness is different from and fatal to the Indian. The two ways, the two streams are never to be united. They are not even to be reconciled. There is no bridge, no canal of connexion.

The sooner we realize, and accept, this, the better, and leave off trying, with fulsome sentimentalism, to render the Indian in our own terms.

The acceptance of the great paradox of human consciousness is the first step to a new accomplishment.

The consciousness of one branch of humanity is the annihilation of the consciousness of another branch. That is, the life of the Indian, his stream of conscious being, is just death to the white man. And we can understand the consciousness of the Indian only in terms of the death of our consciousness.

And let not this be turned into another sentimentalism. Because the same paradox exists between the consciousness of white men and Hindoos or Polynesians or Bantu. It is the eternal paradox of human consciousness. To pretend that all is one stream is to cause chaos and nullity. To pretend to express one stream in terms of another, so as to identify the two, is false and sentimental. The only thing you can do is to have a little Ghost inside you which sees both ways, or even many ways. But a man cannot *belong* to both ways, or to many ways. One man can belong to one great way of consciousness only. He may even change from one way to another. But he cannot go both ways at once. Can't be done.

So that, to understand the Indian conception of entertainment, we have to destroy our own conception.

Perhaps the commonest entertainment among the Indians is singing round the drum, at evening, when the day is over. European peasants will sit round the fire' and sing. But they sing ballads or lyrics, tales about individuals or individual, personal experience. And each individual identifies the emotion of the song with his own emotion.

Or the wild fishermen of the Outer Hebrides will sing in their intense, concentrated way, by the fire. And again, usually, the songs have words. Yet sometimes not. Sometimes the song has merely sounds, and a marvellous melody. It is the seal drifting in to shore on the wave, or the seal-woman, singing low and secret, departing back from the shores of men, through the surf, back to the realm of the outer beasts that rock on the waters and stare through glistening, vivid, mindless eyes.

This is approaching the Indian song. But even this is pictorial, conceptual far beyond the Indian point. The Hebridean still sees himself human, and *outside* the great naturalistic influences, which are the dramatic circumstances of his life.

The Indian, singing, sings without words or vision. Face lifted and sightless, eyes half closed and visionless, mouth open and speechless, the sounds arise in his chest, from the consciousness in the abdomen. He will tell you it is a song of a man coming home from the bear-hunt: or a song to make rain: or a song to make the corn grow: or even, quite modern, the song of the church bell on Sunday morning.

But the man coming home from the bear-hunt is any man, all men, the bear is any bear, every bear, all bear. There is no individual, isolated experience. It is the hunting, tired, triumphant demon of manhood which has won against the squint-eyed demon of all bears. The, experience is generic, non-individual. It is an experience of the human bloodstream, not of the mind or spirit. Hence the subtle incessant, insistent rhythm of the drum, which is pulsated like the heart, and soulless, and unescapable. Hence the strange blind unanimity of the Indian men's voices. The experience is one experience, tribal, of the blood-stream. Hence, to our ears, the absence of melody. Melody is individualized emotion, just as orchestral music is the harmonizing again of many separate, individual emotions or experiences. But the real Indian song is non-individual, and without melody. Strange, clapping, crowing, gurgling sounds, in an unseizable subtle rhythm, the rhythm of the heart in her throes: from a parted entranced mouth, from a chest powerful and free, from an-abdomen where the great blood-stream surges in the dark, and surges in its own generic experiences.

This may mean nothing to you. To the ordinary white ear, the Indian's singing is a rather disagreeable howling of dogs to a tom-tom. But if it rouses no other sensation, it rouses a touch of fear amid hostility. Whatever the spirit of man may be, the blood is basic.

Or take the song to make the corn grow. The dark faces stoop forward, in a strange race darkness. The eyelashes droop a little in the dark, ageless, vulnerable faces. The drum is a heart beating with insistent thuds. And the spirits of the men go out on the ether, vibrating in waves from the hot, dark, intentional blood, seeking the creative presence that hovers for ever in the ether, seeking the identification, following on down the mysterious rhythms of the creative pulse, on and on into the germinating quick of the maize that lies under the ground, there, with the throbbing, pulsing, clapping rhythm that comes from the dark, creative blood in man, to stimulate the tremulous, pulsating protoplasm in the seed-germ, till it throws forth its rhythms of creative energy into rising blades of leaf and stem.

Or take the round dances, round the drum. These may or may not have a name. The dance, anyhow, is primarily a song. All the men sing in unison, as they move with the soft, yet heavy bird-tread which is the whole of the dance. There is no drama. With bodies bent a little forward, shoulders and breasts loose and heavy, feet powerful but soft, the men tread the rhythm into the centre of the earth. The drums keep up the pulsating heart-beat. The men sing in unison, though some will be silent for moments, or even minutes. And for hours, hours it goes on: the round dance.

It has no name. It has no words. It means nothing at all. There is no spectacle, no spectator.

Yet perhaps it is the most stirring sight in the world, in the dark, near the fire, with the drums going, the pine-trees standing still, the everlasting darkness, and the strange lifting and dropping, surging, crowing, gurgling, aah--h--h--ing! of the male voices.

What are they doing? Who knows? But perhaps they are giving themselves again to the pulsing, incalculable fall of the blood, which for ever seeks to fall to the centre of the earth, while the heart like a planet pulsating in an orbit, keeps up the strange, lonely circulating of the separate human existence.

But what we seek, passively, in sleep, they perhaps seek actively, in the round dance. It is the homeward pulling of the blood, as the feet fall in the soft, heavy rhythm, endlessly. It is the dark blood falling back from the mind, from sight and speech and knowing, back to the great central source where is rest and unspeakable renewal. We whites, creatures of spirit, look upon sleep and see only the dreams that lie as debris of the day, mere bits of wreckage from day-consciousness. We never realize the strange falling back of the dark blood into the downward rhythm, the rhythm of pure forgetting and pure renewal.

Or take the little dances round the fire, the mime dances, when two men put on the eagle feathers and take the shield on their arm, and dance the pantomime of a fight, a spear dance. The rhythm is the same, really, the drums keep up the heart-pulsation, the feet the peculiar bird-tread, the soft, heavy, birdlike step that treads as it were towards the centre of the earth. But there is also the subtle leaping towards each other of the two shield-sheltered naked ones, feathered with the power of an eagle. The leaping together, the coming close, the circling, wary, stealthy avoidance and retreat, always on the same rhythm of drum-beats, the same regular, heavy-soft tread of moccasined feet. It is the dance of the naked blood-being, defending his own isolation in the rhythm of the universe. Not skill nor prowess, not heroism. Not man to man. The creature of the isolated, circulating blood-stream dancing in the peril of his own isolation, in the overweening of his own singleness. The glory in power of the man of single existence. The peril of the man whose heart is suspended, like a single red star, in a great and complex universe, following its own lone course round the invisible sun of our own being, amid the strange wandering array of other hearts.

The other men look on. They may or may not sing. And they see themselves in the power and peril of the lonely heart, the creature of the isolated blood-circuit. They see also, subsidiary, the skill, the agility, the swiftness, the daunting onrush that make the warrior. It is practice as well as mystery.

Or take the big, spectacular dances, like the deer dance, the corn dance. The deer dance in the New Year. The people crowded on the roofs of the pueblo: women, children, old men, watching. The two lines of men, hunters, facing one another. And away at the stream which comes running swiftly from among the cotton-wood trees, the watchers, watching eagerly. At last, over the log bridge, two maidens leading the animals: two maidens in their black shawls and wide white deer-skin top-boots, dancing with a slow, delicate-footed rhythm, facing out, then facing in, and shaking their gourd rattles delicately, marking the rhythm as the drums mark it. Following the maidens, all the animals: men in two columns, and each man an animal, leaning forward each on two slim sticks which are his forelegs, with the deer-skin over him, the antlers branching from his head: or the buffalo hide, from whose shaggy mane his bent head peers out: or a black bear, or a wolf. There they come, the two long lines of wild animals: deer, buffalo, bear, wolf, coyote, and at the back, even tiny boys, as foxes, all stepping on those soft, pointed toes, and moving in slow silence under the winter sun, following the slow, swinging progress of the dancing maidens.

Everything is very soft, subtle, delicate. There is none of the hardness of representation. They are not representing something, not even playing. It is a soft, subtle *being* something.

Yet at the same time it is a game, and a very dramatic naïve spectacle. The old men trot softly alongside, laughing, showing all their wrinkles. But they are experiencing a delicate, wild inward delight, participating in the natural mysteries. They tease the little boys under the fox-skins, and the boys, peeping with their round black eyes, are shy and confused. Yet they keep on in the procession, solemnly, as it moves between the ranks of the wild hunters. And all eyes are round with wonder, and the mystery of participation. Amused, too, on the merely human side of themselves. The gay touch of amusement in buffoonery does not in the least detract from the delicate, pulsing wonder of solemnity, which comes from participating in the ceremony itself.

There you have it all, the pantomime, the buffoonery, the human comicalness. But at the same time, quivering bright and wide-eyed in unchangeable delight of solemnity, you have the participating in a natural wonder. The mystery of the wild creatures led from their fastnesses, their wintry retreats and holes in the ground, docilely fascinated by the delicacy and the commanding wistfulness of the maidens who went out to seek them, to seek food in the winter, and who draw after them, in a following, the wild, the timid, the rapacious animals, following in gentle wonder of bewitchment, right into the haunts of men, right into the camp and up to the hunters. The two long lines of wild animals delicately and slowly stepping behind the slow gyration of the two dark-fringed maidens, who shake their gourd rattles in a delicate, quick, three-pulsed rhythm, and never change their wide dark eyes, under the dark fringe. It is the celebration of another triumph, the triumph of the magical wistfulness of women, the wonderful power of her seeking, her yearning, which can draw forth even the bear from his den.

Drama, we are told, has developed out of these ceremonial Glances. Greek drama arose this way.

But from the Indian's ceremonial dance to the Greek's early religious ceremony is still a long step. The Greeks usually had some specified deity, some particular god to whom the ceremony was offered. And this god is the witness, the essential audience of the play. The ceremony is *performed* for the gratification of the god. And here you have the beginning of the theatre, with players and audience.

With the Indians it is different, There is strictly no god. The Indian does not consider himself as created, and therefore external to God, or the creature of God. To the Indian there is no conception of a defined God. Creation is a great flood, for ever flowing, in lovely and terrible waves. In everything, the shimmer of creation, and never the finality of the created. Never the distinction between God and God's creation, or between Spirit and Matter. Everything, everything is the wonderful shimmer of creation, it may be a deadly shimmer like lightning or the anger in the little eyes of the bear, it may be the beautiful shimmer of the moving deer, or the pine-boughs softly swaying under snow. Creation contains the unspeakably terrifying enemy, the unspeakably lovely friend, as the maiden who brings us our food in dead of winter, by her passion of tender wistfulness. Yet even this tender wistfulness is the fearful danger of the wild creatures, deer and bear and buffalo, which find their death in it.

There is, in our sense of the word, no God. But all is godly. There is no Great Mind directing the universe. Yet the mystery of creation, the wonder and fascination of creation shimmers in every leaf and stone, in every thorn and bud, in the fangs of the rattlesnake, and in the soft eyes of a fawn. Things utterly opposite are still pure wonder of creation, the yell of the mountain-lion, and the breeze in the aspen leaves. The Apache warrior in his war-paint, shrieking the war-cry and cutting the throats of old women, still he is part of the mystery of creation. He is godly as the growing corn. And the mystery of creation makes us sharpen the knives and point the arrows in utmost determination against him. It must be so. It is part of the wonder. And to every part of the wonder we must answer in kind.

The Indians accept Jesus on the Cross amid all the rest of the wonders. The presence of Jesus on the Cross, or the pitiful Mary Mother, does not in the least prevent the strange intensity of the war-dance. The brave comes home with a scalp. In the morning he goes to Mass. Two mysteries! The soul of man is the theatre in which every mystery is enacted. Jesus, Mary, the snake-dance, red blood on the knife: it is all the rippling of this untellable flood of creation, which, in a narrow sense, we call Nature.

There is no division between actor and audience. It is all one.

There is no God looking on. The only god there is, is involved all the time in the dramatic wonder and inconsistency of creation. God is immersed, as it were, in creation, not to be separated or distinguished. There can be no Ideal God.

And here finally you see the difference between Indian entertainment and even the earliest form of Greek drama. Right at the beginning of Old World dramatic presentation there was the onlooker, if only in the shape of the God Himself, or the Goddess Herself, to whom the dramatic offering was made. And this God or Goddess resolves, at last, into a Mind occupied by some particular thought or idea. And in the long course of evolution, we ourselves become the gods of our own drama. The spectacle is offered to us. And we sit aloft, enthroned in the Mind, dominated by some one exclusive idea, and we judge the show.

There is absolutely none of this in the Indian dance. There is no God. There is no Onlooker. There is no Mind. There is no dominant idea. And finally, there is no judgement: absolutely no judgement.

The Indian is completely embedded in the wonder of his own drama. It is a drama that has no beginning and no end, it is all-inclusive. It can't be judged, because there is nothing outside it, to judge it.

The mind is there merely as a servant, to keep a man pure and true to the mystery, which is always present. The mind bows down before the creative mystery, even of the atrocious Apache warrior. It judges, not the good and the bad, but the lie and the true. The Apache warrior in all his atrocity, is true to his own creative mystery. And as such, he must he fought. But he cannot be called a *lie* on the face of the earth. Hence he cannot be classed among the abominations, the cowards, and the liars: those who betray the wonder.

The Indian, so long as he is pure, has only two great negative commandments.

Thou shalt not lie.

Thou shalt not be a coward.

Positively, his one commandment is:

Thou shalt acknowledge the wonder.

Evil lies in lying and in cowardice. Wickedness lies in witchcraft; that is, in seeking to prostitute the creative wonder to the individual mind and will, the individual conceit.

And virtue? Virtue lies in the heroic response to the creative wonder, the utmost response. In the man, it is a valiant putting forth of all his strength to meet and to run forward with the wonder. In woman it is the putting forth of all herself in a delicate, marvellous sensitiveness, which draws forth the wonder to herself, and draws the man to the wonder in her, as it drew even the wild animals from the lair of winter.

You see this so plainly in the Indian races. Naked and daubed with clay to hide the nakedness, and to take the anointment of the earth; stuck over with bits of fluff of eagle's down, to be anointed with the power of the air, the youths and men whirl down the racing track, in relays. They are not racing to win a race. They are not racing for a prize. They are not racing to show their prowess.

They are putting forth all their might, all their strength, in a tension that is half anguish, half ecstasy, in the effort to gather into their souls more and more of the creative fire, the creative energy which shall carry their tribe through the year, through the vicissitudes of the months, on, on, in the unending race of humanity along the track of trackless creation. It is the heroic effort, the sacred heroic effort which men must make and must keep on making. As if hurled from a catapult the Indian youth throws himself along the course, working his body strangely incomprehensibly. And when his turn comes again, he hurls himself forward with greater intensity, to greater speed, driving himself, as it were, into the heart of the fire. And the old men along the track encourage him, urge him with their green twigs, laughingly, mockingly, teasingly, but at the same time with an exquisite pure anxiety and concern.

And he walks away at last, his chest lifting and falling heavily, a strange look in his eyes, having run with the changeless god who will give us nothing unless we overtake him.

6 - DANCE OF THE SPROUTING CORN

Pale, dry, baked earth, that blows into dust of fine sand. Low hills of baked pale earth, sinking heavily, and speckled sparsely with dark dots of cedar bushes. A river on the plain of drought, just a cleft of dark, reddish-brown water, almost a flood. And over all, the blue, uneasy, alkaline sky.

A pale, uneven, parched world, where a motor-car rocks and lurches and churns in sand. A world pallid with dryness, inhuman with a faint taste of alkali. Like driving in the bed of a great sea that dried up unthinkable ages ago, and now is drier than any other dryness, yet still reminiscent of the bottom of the sea, sandhills sinking, and straight, cracked mesas, like cracks in the dry-mud bottom of the sea.

So, the mud church standing discreetly outside, just outside the pueblo, not to see too much. And on its façade of mud, under the timbered mud-eaves, two speckled horses rampant, painted by the Indians, a red piebald and a black one.

Swish! Over the logs of the ditch-bridge, where brown water is flowing full. There below is the pueblo, dried mud like mud-pie houses, all squatting in a jumble, prepared to crumble into dust and be invisible, dust to dust returning, earth to earth.

That they don't crumble is the mystery. That these little squarish mud-heaps endure for centuries after centuries, while Greek marble tumbles asunder, and cathedrals totter, is the wonder. But then, the naked human hand with a bit of new soft mud is quicker than time, and defies the centuries.

Roughly the low, square, mud-pie houses make a wide street where all is naked earth save a doorway or a window with a pale-blue sash. At the end of the street, turn again into a parallel wide, dry street. And there, in the dry, oblong aridity, there tosses a small forest that is alive: and thud--thud--thud goes the drum, and the deep sound of men singing is like the deep soughing of the wind, in the depths of a wood.

You realize that you had heard the drum from the distance, also the deep, distant roar and boom of the singing, but that you had not heeded, as you don't heed the wind.

It all tosses like young, agile trees in a wind. This is the dance of the sprouting corn, and everybody holds a little, beating branch of green pine. Thud--thud--thud--thud--thud! goes the drum, heavily the men hop and hop and hop, sway, sway, sway, sway go the little branches of green pine. It tosses like a little forest, and the deep sound of men's singing is like the booming and tearing of a wind deep inside a forest. They are dancing the Spring Corn Dance.

This is the Wednesday after Easter, after Christ Risen and the corn germinated. They dance on Monday and on Tuesday. Wednesday is the third and last dance of this green resurrection.

You realize the long line of dancers, and a solid cluster of men singing near the drum. You realize the intermittent black-and-white fantasy of the hopping Koshare, the jesters, the Delight-Makers. You become aware of the ripple of bells on the knee-garters of the dancers, a continual pulsing ripple of little bells; and of the sudden wild, whooping yells from near the drum. Then you become aware of the seed-like shudder of the gourd-rattles, as the dance changes, and the slaying of the tufts of green pine-twigs stuck behind the arms of all the dancing men, in the broad green arm-bands.

Gradually come through to you the black, stable solidity of the dancing women, who poise like solid shadow, one woman behind each rippling, leaping male. The long, silky black hair of the women streaming down their backs, and the equally long, streaming, gleaming hair of the males, loose over broad, naked, orange-brown shoulders.

Then the faces, the impassive, rather fat, golden-brown faces of the women, with eyes cast down, crowned above with the green tableta, like a flat tiara. Something strange and noble about the impassive, barefoot women in the short black cassocks, as they subtly tread the dance, scarcely moving, and yet edging rhythmically along, swaying from each hand the green spray of pine-twig out--out--out, to the thud of the drum, immediately behind the leaping fox-skin of the men dancers. And all the emerald-green, painted *tabletas*, the flat wooden tiaras shaped like a castle gateway, rise steady and noble from the soft, slightly bowed heads of the women, held by a band under the chin. All the *tabletas* down the line, emerald green, almost steady, while the bright black heads of the men leap softly up and down, between.

Bit by bit you take it in. You cannot get a whole impression, save of some sort of wood tossing, a little forest of trees in motion, with gleaming black hair and gold-ruddy breasts that somehow do not destroy the illusion of forest.

When you look at the women, you forget the men. The bare-armed, bare-legged, barefoot women with streaming hair and lofty green tiaras, impassive, downward-looking faces, twigs swaying outwards from subtle, rhythmic wrists; women clad in the black, prehistoric short gown fastened over one shoulder, leaving the other shoulder bare, and showing at the arm-place a bit of pink or white undershirt; belted also round the waist with a woven woollen sash, scarlet and green on the hand-woven black cassock. The noble, slightly submissive bending of the tiara-ed head. The subtle measure of the hare, breathing, bird-like feet, that are flat, and seem to cleave to earth softly, and softly lift away. The continuous outward swaying of the pine-sprays.

But when you look at the men, you forget the women. The men are naked to the waist, and ruddy-golden, and in the rhythmic hopping leap of the dance their breasts shake downwards, as the strong, heavy body comes down, down, down, down, in the downward plunge of the dance. The black hair streams loose and living down their backs, the black brows are level, the black eyes look out unchanging from under the silky lashes. They are handsome, and absorbed with a deep rhythmic absorption, which still leaves them awake and aware. Down, down, down they drop, on the heavy, ceaseless leap of the dance, and the great necklaces of shell-cores spring on the naked breasts, the neck-shell flaps up and down, the short white kilt of woven stuff, with the heavy woollen embroidery, green and red and black, opens and shuts slightly to the strong lifting of the knees: the heavy whitish cords that hang from the kilt-band at the side sway and coil for ever down the side of the right leg, down to the ankle, the bells on the red-woven garters under the knees ripple without end, and the feet, in buckskin boots furred round the ankle with a beautiful band of skunk fur, black with a white tip, come down with a lovely, heavy, soft precision, first one, then the other, dropping always plumb to earth. Slightly bending forward, a black gourd rattle in the right hand, a small green bough in the left, the dancer dances the eternal drooping leap, that brings his life down, down, down, down from the mind, down from the broad, beautiful shaking breast, down to the powerful pivot of the knees, then to the ankles, and plunges deep from the ball of the foot into the earth, towards the earth's red centre, where these men belong, as is signified by the red earth with which they are smeared.

And meanwhile, the shell-cores from the Pacific sway up and down, ceaselessly on their breasts.

Mindless, without effort, under the hot sun, unceasing, yet never perspiring nor even breathing heavily, they dance on and on. Mindless, yet still listening, observing. They hear the deep, surging singing of the bunch of old men, like a great wind soughing. They hear the cries and yells of the man waving his bough by the drum. They catch the word of the song, and at a moment, shudder the black rattles, wheel, and the line breaks, women from men, they thread across to a new formation. And as the men wheel round, their black hair gleams and shakes, and the long fox-skin sways, like a tail. And always, when they form into line again, it is a beautiful long straight line, flexible as life, but straight as rain.

The men round the drum are old, or elderly. They are all in a bunch, and they wear day dress, loose cotton drawers, pink or white cotton shirt, hair tied up behind with the red cords, and banded round the head with a strip of pink rag, or white rag, or blue. There they are, solid like a cluster of bees, their black heads with the pink rag circles all close together, swaying their pine-twigs with rhythmic, wind-swept hands, dancing slightly, mostly on the right foot, ceaselessly, and singing, their black bright eyes absorbed, their dark lips pushed out, while the deep strong sound rushes like wind, and the unknown words form themselves in the dark.

Suddenly the solitary man pounding the drum swings his drum round, and begins to pound on the other end, on a higher note, pang--pang--pang! instead of the previous brumm! brumm! brumm! of the bass note. The watchful man next the drummer yells and waves lightly, dancing on bird-feet. The Koshare make strange, eloquent gestures to the sky.

And again the gleaming bronze-and-dark men dancing in the rows shudder their rattles, break the rhythm, change into a queer, beautiful two-step, the long lines suddenly curl into rings, four rings of dancers, the leaping, gleaming-seeming men between the solid, subtle, submissive blackness of the women who are crowned with emerald-green tiaras, all going subtly round in rings. Then slowly they change again, and form a star. Then again, unmingling, they come back into rows.

And all the while, all the while the naked Koshare are threading about. Of bronze-and-dark men-dancers there are some forty-two, each with a dark, crowned woman attending him like a shadow. The old men, the bunch of singers in shirts and tied-up black hair, are about sixty in number, or sixty-four. The Koshare are about twenty-four.

They are slim and naked, daubed with black and white earth, their hair daubed white and gathered upwards to a great knot on top of the head, whence springs a tuft of corn-husks, dry corn-leaves. Though they wear nothing but a little black square cloth, front and back, at their middle, they do not seem naked, for some are white with black spots, like a leopard, and some have broad black lines or zigzags on their smeared bodies, and all their faces are blackened with triangle or lines till they look like weird masks. Meanwhile their hair, gathered straight up and daubed white and sticking up from the top of the head with corn-husks, completes the fantasy. They are anything but natural. Like blackened ghosts of a dead corn-cob, tufted at the top.

And all the time, running like queer spotted dogs, they weave nakedly, through the unheeding dance, comical, weird, dancing the dance-step naked and fine, prancing through the lines, up and down the lines, and making fine gestures with their flexible hands, calling something down from the sky, calling something up from the earth, and dancing forward all the time. Suddenly as they catch a word from the singers, name of a star, of a wind, a name for the sun, for a cloud, their hands soar up and gather in the air, soar down with a slow motion. And again, as they catch a word that means earth, earth deeps, water within the earth, or red-earth-quickening, the hands flutter softly down, and draw up the water, draw up the earth-quickening, earth to sky, sky to earth, influences above to influences below, to meet in the germ-quick of corn, where life is.

And as they dance, the Koshare watch the dancing men. And if a fox-skin is coming loose at the belt, they fasten it as the man dances, or they stoop and tie another man's shoe. For the dancer must not hesitate to the end.

And then, after some forty minutes,' the drum stops. Slowly the dancers file into one line, woman behind man, and move away, threading towards their kiva, with no sound but the tinkle of knee-bells in the silence.

But at the same moment the thud of an unseen drum, from beyond, the soughing of deep song approaching from the unseen. It is the other half, the other half of the tribe coming to continue the dance. They appear round the kiva--one Koshare and one dancer leading the rows, the old men all abreast, singing already in a great strong burst.

So, from ten o'clock in the morning till about four in the afternoon, first one-half then the other. Till at last, as the day wanes, the two halves meet, and the two singings like two great winds surge one past the other, and the thicket of the dance becomes a real forest. It is the close of the third day.

Afterwards, the men and women crowd on the roofs of the two low round towers, the kivas, while the Koshare run round jesting and miming, and taking big offerings from the women, loaves of bread and cakes of blue-maize meal. Women come carrying big baskets of bread and guayava, on two hands, an offering.

And the mystery of germination, not procreation, but *putting forth*, resurrection, life springing within the seed, is accomplished. The sky has its fire, its waters, its stars, its wandering electricity, its winds, its fingers of cold. The earth has its reddened body, its invisible hot heart, its inner waters and many juices and unaccountable stuffs. Between them all, the little seed: and also man, like a seed that is busy and aware. And from the heights and from the depths man, the caller, calls: man, the knower, brings down the influences and brings up the influences, with his knowledge: man, so vulnerable, so subject, and yet even in his vulnerability and subjection, a master, commands the invisible influences and is obeyed. Commands in that song, in that rhythmic energy of dance, in that still-submissive mockery of the Koshare. And he accomplishes his end, as master. He partakes in the springing of the corn, in the rising and budding and Baring of the corn. And when he eats his bread at last, he recovers all he once sent forth, and partakes again of the energies he called to the corn, from out of the wide universe.

7 - THE HOPI SNAKE DANCE

The Hopi country is in Arizona, next the Navajo country, and some seventy miles north of the Santa Fé railroad. The Hopis are Pueblo Indians, village Indians, so their reservation is not large. It consists of a square track of greyish, unappetizing desert, out of which rise three tall arid mesas, broken off in ragged pallid rock. On the top of the mesas perch the ragged, broken, greyish pueblos, identical with the mesas on which they stand.

The nearest village, Walpi, stands in half-ruin high, high on a narrow rock-top where no leaf of life ever was tender. It is all grey, utterly grey, utterly pallid stone and dust, and very narrow. Below it all the stark light of the dry Arizona sun.

Walpi is called the 'first mesa'. And it is at the far edge of Walpi you see the withered beaks and claws and bones of sacrificed eagles, in a rock-cleft under the sky. They sacrifice an eagle each year, on the brink, by rolling him out and crushing him so as to shed no blood. Then they drop his remains down the dry cleft in the promontory's farthest grey tip.

The trail winds on, utterly bumpy and horrible, for thirty miles, past the second mesa, where Chimopova is, on to the third mesa. And on the Sunday afternoon of 17th August black automobile after automobile lurched and crawled across the grey desert, where low, grey, sage-scrub was coming to pallid yellow. Black hood followed crawling after black hood, like a funeral cortège. The motor-cars, with all the tourists wending their way to the third and farthest mesa, thirty miles across this dismal desert where an odd water-windmill spun, and odd patches of corn blew in the strong desert wind, like dark-green women with fringed shawls blowing and fluttering, not far from the foot of the great, grey, up-piled mesa.

The snake dance (I am told) is held once a year, on each of the three mesas in succession. This year of grace 1924 it was to be held in Hotevilla, the last village on the farthest western tip of the third mesa.

On and on bumped the cars. The lonely second mesa lay in the distance. On and on, to the ragged ghost of the third mesa.

The third mesa has two main villages, Oraibi, which is on the near edge, and Hotevilla, on the far. Up scrambles the car, on all its four legs, like a black-beetle straddling past the school-house and store down below, up the bare rock and over the changeless boulders, with a surge and a sickening lurch to the sky-brim, where stands the rather foolish church. Just beyond, dry, grey, ruined, and apparently abandoned, Oraibi, its few ragged stone huts. All these cars come all this way, and apparently nobody at home.

You climb still, up the shoulder of rock, a few more miles, across the lofty, wind-swept mesa, and so you come to Hote-villa, where the dance is, and where already hundreds of motor-cars are herded in an official camping-ground, among the piñon bushes.

Hotevilla is a tiny little village of grey little houses, raggedly built with undressed stone and mud around a little oblong *plaza*, and partly in ruins. One of the chief two-storey houses on the small square is a ruin, with big square window-holes.

It is a parched, grey country of snakes and eagles, pitched up against the sky. And a few dark-faced, short, thickly built Indians have their few peach trees among the sand, their beans and squashes on the naked sand under the sky, their springs of brackish water.

Three thousand people came to see the little snake dance this year, over miles of desert and bumps. Three thousand, of all sorts, cultured people from New York, Californians, onward-pressing tourists, cowboys, Navajo Indians, even Negroes; fathers, mothers, children, of all ages, colours, sizes of stoutness, dimensions of curiosity.

What had they come for? Mostly to see men hold *live rattlesnakes* in their mouths. *'I never did see a rattlesnake and I'm crazy to see one!'* cried a girl with bobbed hair.

There you have it. People trail hundreds of miles, avidly, to see this circus-performance of men handling live rattlesnakes that may bite them any minute--even do bite them. Some show, that!

There is the other aspect, of the ritual dance. One may look on from the angle of culture, as one looks on while Anna Pavlova dances with the Russian Ballet.

Or there is still another point of view, the religious. Before the snake dance begins, on the Monday, and the spectators are packed thick on the ground round the square, and in the window-holes, and on all the roofs, all sorts of people greedy with curiosity, a little speech is made to them all, asking the audience to be silent and respectful, as this is a sacred religious ceremonial of the Hopi Indians, and not a public entertainment. Therefore, please, no clapping or cheering or applause, but remember you are, as it were, in a church.

The audience accepts the implied rebuke in good faith, and looks round with a grin at the 'church'. But it is a good-humoured, very decent crowd, ready to respect any sort of feelings. And the Indian with his 'religion' is a sort of public pet.

From the cultured point of view, the Hopi snake dance is almost nothing, not much more than a circus turn, or the games that children play in the street. It has none of the impressive beauty of the Corn Dance at Santo Domingo, for example. The big pueblos of Zuni, Santo Domingo, Taos have a cultured instinct which is not revealed in the Hopi snake dance. This last is uncouth rather than beautiful, and rather uncouth in its touch of horror. Hence the thrill, and the crowd.

As a cultured spectacle, it is a circus turn: men actually dancing round with snakes, poisonous snakes, dangling from their mouths.

And as a religious ceremonial: well, you can either be politely tolerant like the crowd to the Hopis; or you must have some spark of understanding of the sort of religion implied.

'Oh, the Indians,' I heard a woman say, they believe we are all brothers, the snakes are the Indians' brothers, and the Indians are the snakes' brothers. The Indians would never hurt the snakes, they won't hurt any animal. So the snakes won't bite the Indians. They are all brothers, and none of them hurt anybody.'

This sounds very nice, only more Hindoo than Hopi. The dance itself does not convey much sense of fraternal communion. It is not in the least like St Francis preaching to the birds.

The animistic religion, as we call it, is not the religion of the Spirit. A religion of spirits, yes. But not of Spirit. There is no One Spirit. There is no One God. There is no Creator. There is strictly no God at all: because all is alive. In our conception of religion there exists God and His Creation: two things. We are creatures of God, therefore we pray to God as the Father, the Saviour, the Maker.

But strictly, in the religion of aboriginal America, there is no Father, and no Maker. There is the great living source of life: say the Sun of existence: to which you can no more pray than you can pray to Electricity. And emerging from this Sun are the great potencies, the invincible influences which make shine and warmth and rain. From these great interrelated potencies of rain and heat and thunder emerge the seeds of life itself, corn, and creatures like snakes. And beyond these, men, persons. But all emerge separately. There is no oneness, no sympathetic identifying oneself with the rest. The law of isolation is heavy on every creature.

Now the Sun, the rain, the shine, the thunder, they are alive. But they are not persons or people. They are alive. They are manifestations of living activity. But they are not personal Gods.

Everything lives. Thunder lives, and rain lives, and sunshine lives. But not in the personal sense.

How is man to get himself into relation with the vast living convulsions of rain and thunder and sun, which are conscious and alive and potent, but like vastest of beasts, inscrutable and incomprehensible. How is man to get himself into relation with these, the vastest of cosmic beasts?

It is the problem of the ages of man. Our religion says the cosmos is Matter, to be conquered by the Spirit of Man. The yogi, the fakir, the saint try conquest by abnegation and by psychic powers. The real conquest of the cosmos is made by science.

The American-Indian sees no division into Spirit and Matter, God and not-God. Everything is alive, though not personally so. Thunder is neither Thor nor Zeus. Thunder is the vast living thunder asserting itself like some incomprehensible monster, or some huge reptile-bird of the pristine cosmos.

How to conquer the dragon-mouthed thunder! How to capture the feathered rain!

We make reservoirs, and irrigation ditches and artesian wells. We make lightning conductors, and build vast electric plants. We say it is a matter of science, energy, force.

But the Indian says No! It all lives. We must approach it fairly, with profound respect, but also with desperate courage. Because man must conquer the cosmic monsters of living thunder and live rain. The rain that slides down from its source, and ebbs back subtly, with a strange energy generated between its coming and going, an energy which, even to our science, is of life: this, man has to conquer. The serpent-striped, feathery Rain.

We made the conquest by dams and reservoirs and windmills. The Indian, like the old Egyptian, seeks to make the conquest from the mystic will within him, pitted against the Cosmic Dragon.

We must remember, to the animistic vision there is no perfect God behind us, who created us from his knowledge, and foreordained all things. No such God. Behind lies only the terrific, terrible, crude Source, the mystic Sun, the well-head of all things. From this mystic Sun emanate the Dragons, Rain, Wind, Thunder Shine, Light. The Potencies of Powers. These bring forth Earth, then reptiles, birds, and fishes.

The Potencies are not Gods. They are Dragons. The Sun of Creation itself is a dragon most terrible, vast, and most powerful, yet even so, less in being than we. The only gods on earth are men. For gods, like man, do not exist beforehand. They are created and evolved gradually, with aeons of effort, out of the fire and smelting of life. They are the highest thing created, smelted between the furnace of the Life-Sun, and beaten on the anvil of the rain, with hammers or thunder and bellows of rushing wind. The cosmos is a great furnace, a dragon's den, where the heroes and demi-gods, men, forge themselves into being. It is a vast and violent matrix, where souls form like diamonds in earth, under extreme pressure.

So that gods are the outcome, not the origin. And the best gods that have resulted, so far, are men. But gods frail as flowers; which have also the godliness of things that have won perfection out of the terrific dragon-clutch of the cosmos. Men are frail as flowers. Man is as a flower, rain can kill him or succour him, heat can flick him with a bright tail, and destroy him: or, on the other hand, it can softly call him into existence, out of the egg of chaos. Man is delicate as a flower, godly beyond flowers, and his lordship is a ticklish business.

He has to conquer, and hold his own, and again conquer all the time. Conquer the powers of the cosmos. To us, science is our religion of conquest. Hence through science, we are the conquerors and resultant gods of our earth. But to the Indian, the so-called mechanical processes do not exist. All lives. And the conquest is made by the means of the living will.

This is the religion of all aboriginal America. Peruvian, Aztec, Athabascan: perhaps the aboriginal religion of all the word. In Mexico, men fell into horror of the crude, pristine gods, the dragons. But to the pueblo Indian, the most terrible dragon is still somewhat gentle-hearted.

This brings us back to the Hopi. He has the hardest task, the stubbornest destiny. Some inward fate drove him to the top of these parched mesas, all rocks and eagles, sand and snakes, and wind and sun and alkali. These he had to conquer. Not merely, as we should put it, the natural conditions of the place. But the mysterious life-spirit that reigned there. The eagle and the snake.

It is a destiny as well as another. The destiny of the animistic soul of man, instead of our destiny of Mind and Spirit. We have undertaken the scientific conquest of forces, of natural conditions. It has been comparatively easy, and we are victors. Look at our black motor-cars like beetles working up the rock-face at Oraibi. Look at our three thousand tourists gathered to gaze at the twenty lonely men who dance in the tribe's snake dance!

The Hopi sought the conquest by means of the mystic, living will that is in man, pitted against the living will of the dragon-cosmos. The Egyptians long ago made a partial conquest by the same means. We have made a partial conquest by other means. Our corn doesn't fail us: we have no seven years' famine, and apparently need never have. But the other thing fails us, the strange inward sun of life; the pellucid monster of the rain never shows us his stripes. To us, heaven switches on daylight, or turns on the shower-bath. We little gods are gods of the machine only. It is our highest. Our cosmos is a great *ennui*. And we die of ennui. A subtle dragon stings us in the midst of plenty. *Quos vult perdere Deus, dementat prius.*

On the Sunday evening is a first little dance in the plaza at Hotevilla, called the Antelope dance. There is the hot, sandy, oblong little place, with a tuft of green cotton-wood boughs stuck like a plume at the south end, and on the floor at the foot of the green, a little lid of a trap-door. They say the snakes are under there.

They say that the twelve officiating men of the snake clan of the tribe have for nine days been hunting snakes in the rocks. They have been performing the mysteries for nine days, in the kiva, and for two days they have fasted completely. All these days they have tended the snakes, washed them with repeated lustrations, soothed them, and exchanged spirits with them. The spirit of man soothing and seeking and making interchange with the spirits of the snakes. For the snakes are more rudimentary, nearer to the great convulsive powers. Nearer to the nameless Sun, more knowing in the slanting tracks of the rain, the pattering of the invisible feet of the rain-monster from the sky. The snakes are man's next emissaries to the rain-gods. The snakes lie nearer to the source of potency, the dark, lurking, intense sun at the centre of the earth. For to the cultured animist, and the pueblo Indian is such, the earth's dark centre holds its dark sun, our source of isolated being, round which our world coils its folds like a great snake. The snake is nearer the dark sun, and cunning of it.

They say--people say--that rattlesnakes are not travellers. They haunt the same spots on earth, and die there. It is said also that the snake priest (so-called) of the Hopi probably capture the same snakes year after year.

Be that as it may. At sundown before the real dance, there is the little dance called the Antelope Dance. We stand and wait on a house-roof. Behind us is tethered an eagle; rather dishevelled he sits on the coping, and looks at us in unutterable resentment. See him, and see how much 'brotherhood' the Indian feels with animals--at best the silent tolerance that acknowledges dangerous difference. We wait without event. There are no drums, no announcements. Suddenly into the *plaza*, with rude, intense movements, hurried a little file of men. They are smeared all with grey and black, and are naked save for little kilts embroidered like the sacred dance-kilts in other pueblos, red and green and black on a white fibre-cloth. The fox-skins hangs behind. The feet of the dancers are pure ash-grey. Their hair is long.

The first is a heavy old man with heavy, long, wild grey hair and heavy fringe. He plods intensely forward in the silence, followed in a sort of circle by the other grey-smeared, longhaired, naked, concentrated men. The oldest men are first: the last is a short-haired boy of fourteen or fifteen. There are only eight men--the so-called antelope priests. They pace round in a circle, rudely, absorbedly, till the first heavy, intense old man with his massive grey hair flowing, comes to the lid on the ground, near the tuft of kiva-boughs. He rapidly shakes from the hollow of his right hand a little white meal on the lid, stamps heavily, with naked right foot, on the meal, so the wood resounds, and paces heavily forward. Each man, to the boy, shakes meal, stamps, paces absorbedly on in the circle, comes to the lid again, shakes meal, stamps, paces absorbedly on, comes a third time to the lid, or trap-door, and this time spits on the lid, stamps, and goes on. And this time the eight men file away behind the lid, between it and the tuft of green boughs. And there they stand in a line, their backs to the kivatuft of green; silent, absorbed, bowing a little to the ground.

Suddenly paces with rude haste another file of men. They are naked, and smeared with red 'medicine', with big black lozenges of smeared paint on their backs. Their wild heavy hair hangs loose, the old, heavy, grey-haired men go first, then the middle-aged, then the young men, then last, two short-haired, slim boys, schoolboys. The hair of the young men, growing after school, is bobbed round.

The grown men are all heavily built, rather short, with heavy but shapely flesh, and rather straight sides. They have not the archaic slim waists of the Taos Indians. They have archaic squareness, and a sensuous heaviness. Their very hair is black, massive, heavy. These are the so-called snake-priests, men of the snake clan. And tonight they are eleven in number.

They pace rapidly round, with that heavy wild silence of concentration characteristic of them, and cast meal and stamp upon the lid, cast meal and stamp in the second round, come round and spit and stamp in the third. For to the savage, the animist, to spit may be a kind of blessing, a communion, a sort of embrace.

The eleven snake-priests form silently in a row, facing the eight grey smeared antelope-priests across the little lid, and bowing forward a little, to earth. Then the antelope-priests, bending forward, begin a low, sombre chant, or call, that sounds wordless, only a deep, low-toned, secret Ay-a! Ay-a! Ay-a! And they bend from right to left, giving two shakes to the little, flat, white rattle in their left hand, at each shake, and stamping the right foot in heavy rhythm. In their right hand, that held the meal, is grasped a little skin bag, perhaps also containing meal.

They lean from right to left, two seed-like shakes of the rattle each time and the heavy rhythmic stamp of the foot, and the low, sombre, secretive chant-call each time. It is a strange low sound, such as we never hear, and it reveals how deep, how deep the men are in the mystery they are practising, how sunk deep below our world, to the world of snakes, and dark ways in the earth, where the roots of corn, and where the little rivers of unchannelled, uncreated life-passion run like dark, trickling lightning, to the roots of the corn and to the feet and loins of men, from the earth's innermost dark sun. They are calling in the deep, almost silent snake-language, to the snakes and the rays of dark emission from the earth's inward 'Sun'.

At this moment, a silence falls on the whole crowd of listeners. It is that famous darkness and silence of Egypt, the touch of the other mystery. The deep concentration of the 'priests' conquers for a few seconds our white-faced flippancy, and we hear only the deep Hah-hà! Hah-ha! speaking to snakes and the earth's inner core.

This lasts a minute or two. Then the antelope-priests stand bowed and still, and the snake-priests take up the swaying and the deep chant, that sometimes is so low, it is like a mutter underground, inaudible. The rhythm is crude, the swaying unison is all uneven. Culturally, there is nothing. If it were not for that mystic, dark-sacred concentration.

Several times in turn, the two rows of daubed, long-haired, insunk men facing one another take up the swaying and the chant. Then that too is finished. There is a break in the formation. A young snake-priest takes up something that may be a corn-cob--perhaps an antelope-priest hands it to him--and comes forward, with an old, heavy, but still shapely snake-priest behind him dusting his shoulders with the feathers, eagle-feathers presumably, which are the Indians' hollow prayer-sticks. With the heavy, stamping hop they move round in the previous circle, the young priest holding the cob curiously, and the old priest prancing strangely at the young priest's hack, in a sort of incantation, and brushing the heavy young shoulders delicately with the prayer-feathers. It is the God-vibration that enters us from behind, and is transmitted to the hands, from the hands to the corn-cob. Several young priests emerge, with the bowed heads and the cob in their hands and the heavy older priests hanging over them behind. They tread round the rough curve and come back to the kiva, take perhaps another cob, and tread round again.

That is all. In ten or fifteen minutes it is over. The two files file rapidly and silently away. A brief, primitive performance.

The crowd disperses. They were not many people. There were no venomous snakes on exhibition, so the mass had nothing to come for. And therefore the curious immersed intensity of the priests was able to conquer the white crowd.

By afternoon of the next day the three thousand people had massed in the little *plaza*, secured themselves places on the roof and in the window-spaces, everywhere, till the small pueblo seemed built of people instead of stones. All sorts of people, hundreds and hundreds of white women, all in breeches like half-men, hundreds and hundreds of men who had been driving motor-cars, then many Navajos, the women in their full, long skirts and tight velvet bodices, the men rather lanky, long-waisted, real nomads. In the hot sun and the wind which blows the sand every day, every day in volumes round the corners, the three thousand tourists sat for hours, waiting for the show. The Indian policeman cleared the central oblong, in front of the kiva. The front rows of onlookers sat thick on the ground. And at last, rather early, because of the masses awaiting them, suddenly, silently, in the same rude haste, the antelope-priests filed absorbedly in, and made the rounds over the lid, as before. Today, the eight antelope-priests were very grey. Their feet ashed pure grey, like suède soft boots: and their lower jaw was pure suède grey, while the rest of their face was blackish. With that pale-grey jaw, they looked like corpse-faces with swathing-bands. And all their bodies ash-grey smeared, with smears of black, and a black cloth today at the loins.

They made their rounds, and took their silent position behind the lid, with backs to the green tuft: an unearthly grey row of men with little skin bags in their hands. They were the lords of shadow, the intermediate twilight, the place of afterlife and before-life, where house the winds of change. Lords of the mysterious, fleeting power of change.

Suddenly, with abrupt silence, in paced the snake-priests, headed by the same heavy man with solid grey hair like iron. Today they were twelve men, from the old one, down to the slight, short-haired, erect boy of fourteen. Twelve men, two for each of the six worlds, or quarters: east, north, south, west, above, and below. And today they were in a queer ecstasy. Their faces were black, showing the whites of the eyes. And they wore small black loin-aprons. They were the hot living men of the darkness, lords of the earth's inner rays, the black sun of the earth's vital core, from which dart the speckled snakes, like beams.

Round they went, in rapid, uneven, silent absorption, the three rounds. Then in a row they faced the eight ash-grey men, across the lid. All kept their heads bowed towards earth, except the young boys.

Then, in the intense, secret, muttering chant the grey men began their leaning from right to left, shaking the hand, one-two, one-two, and bowing the body each time from right to left, left to right, above the lid in the ground, under which were the snakes. And their low, deep, mysterious voices spoke to the spirits under the earth, not to men above the earth.

But the crowd was on tenterhooks for the snakes, and could hardly wait for the mummery to cease. There was an atmosphere of inattention and impatience. But the chant and the swaying passed from the grey men to the black-faced men, and back again, several times.

This was finished. The formation of the lines broke up. There was a slight crowding to the centre, round the lid. The old antelope-priest (so called) was stooping. And before the crowd could realize anything else a young priest emerged, bowing reverently, with the neck of a pale, delicate rattlesnake held between his teeth, the little, naïve, bird-like head of the rattlesnake quite still, near the black cheek, and the long, pale, yellowish, spangled body of the snake dangling like some thick, beautiful cord. On passed the black-faced young priest, with the wondering snake dangling from his mouth, pacing in the original circle, while behind him, leaping almost on his shoulders, was the oldest heavy priest, dusting the young man's shoulders with the feather-prayer-sticks, in an intense, earnest anxiety of concentration such as I have only seen in the old Indian men during a religious dance.

Came another young black-faced man out of the confusion, with another snake dangling and writhing a little from his mouth, and an elder priest dusting him from behind with the feathers: and then another, and another: till it was all confusion, probably, of six, and then four young priests with snakes dangling from their mouths, going round, apparently, three times in the circle. At the end of the third round the young priest stooped and delicately laid his snake on the earth, waving him away, away, as it were, into the world. He must not wriggle back to the kiva bush.

And after wondering a moment, the pale, delicate snake steered away with a rattlesnake's beautiful movement, rippling and looping, with the small, sensitive head lifted like antennae, across the sand to the massed audience squatting solid on the ground around. Like soft, watery lightning went the wondering snake at the crowd. As he came nearer, the people began to shrink aside, half-mesmerized. But they betrayed no exaggerated fear. And as the little snake drew very near, up rushed one of the two black-faced young priests who held the snake-stick, poised a moment over the snake, in the prayer-concentration of reverence which is at the same time conquest, and snatched the pale, long creature delicately from the ground, waving him in a swoop over the heads of the seated crowd, then delicately smoothing down the length of the snake with his left hand, stroking and smoothing and soothing the long, pale, bird-like thing; and returning with it to the kiva, handed it to one of the grey-jawed antelope-priests.

Meanwhile, all the time, the other young priests were emerging with a snake dangling from their mouths. The boy had finished his rounds. He launched his rattlesnake on the ground, like a ship, and like a ship away it steered. In a moment, after it went one of those two black-faced priests who carried snake-sticks and were the snake-catchers. As it neared the crowd, very close, he caught it up and waved it dramatically, his eyes glaring strangely out of his black face. And in the interim that youngest boy had been given a long, handsome bull-snake, by the priest at the hole under the kiva boughs. The bull-snake is not poisonous. It is a constrictor. This one was six feet long, with a sumptuous pattern. It waved its pale belly, and pulled its neck out of the boy's mouth. With two hands he put it back. It pulled itself once more free. Again he got it back, and managed to hold it. And then as he went round in his looping circle, it coiled its handsome folds twice round his knee. He stooped, quietly, and as quietly as if he were untying his garter, he unloosed the folds. And all the time, an old priest was intently brushing the boy's thin straight shoulders with the feathers. And all the time, the snakes seemed strangely gentle, naïve, wondering and almost willing, almost in harmony with the man. Which of course was the sacred aim. While the boy's expression remained quite still and simple, as it were candid, in a candour where he and the snake should be in unison. The only dancers who showed signs of being wrought-up were the two young snake-catchers, and one of these, particularly, seemed in a state of actor-like uplift, rather ostentatious. But the old priests had that immersed, religious intentness which is like a spell, something from another world.

The young boy launched his bull-snake. It wanted to go back to the kiva. The snake-catcher drove it gently forward. Away it went, towards the crowd, and at the last minute was caught up into the air. Then this snake was handed to an old man sitting on the ground in the audience, in the front row. He was an old Hopi of the Snake clan.

Snake after snake had been carried round in the circles, dangling by the neck from the mouths of one young priest or another, and writhing and swaying slowly, with the small, delicate snake-head held as if wondering and listening. There had been some very large rattlesnakes, unusually large, two or three handsome bull-snakes, and some racers, whipsnakes. All had been launched, after their circuits in the mouth, all had been caught up by the young priests with the snake-sticks, one or two had been handed to old-snake clan men in the audience, who sat holding them in their arms as men hold a kitten. The most of the snakes, however, had been handed to the grey antelope-men who stood in the row with their backs to the kiva bush. Till some of these ash-smeared men held armfuls of snakes, hanging over their arms like wet washing. Some of the snakes twisted and knotted round one another, showing pale bellies.

Yet most of them hung very still and docile. Docile, almost sympathetic, so that one was struck only by their clean, slim length of snake nudity, their beauty, like soft, quiescent lightning. They were so clean, because they had been washed and anointed and lustrated by the priests, in the days they had been in the kiva.

At last all the snakes had been mouth-carried in the circuits, and had made their little outrunning excursion to the crowd, and had been handed back to the priests in the rear. And now the Indian policemen, Hopi and Navajo, began to clear away the crowd that sat on the ground, five or six rows deep, around the small *plaza*. The snakes were all going to be set free on the ground. We must clear away.

We recoiled to the farther end of the *plaza*. There, two Hopi women were scattering white corn-meal on the sandy ground. And thither came the two snake-catchers, almost at once, with their arms full of snakes. And before we who stood had realized it, the snakes were all writhing and squirming on the ground, in the white dust of meal, a couple of yards from our feet. Then immediately, before they could writhe clear of each other and steer away, they were gently, swiftly snatched up again, and with their arms full of snakes, the two young priests went running out of the *plaza*.

We followed slowly, wondering, towards the western, or north-western edge of the mesa. There the mesa dropped steeply, and a broad trail wound down to the vast hollow of desert brimmed up with strong evening light, up out of which jutted a perspective of sharp rock and further mesas and distant sharp mountains: the great, hollow, rock-wilderness space of that part of Arizona, submerged in light.

Away down the trail, small, dark, naked, rapid figures with arms held close, went the two young men, running swiftly down to the hollow level, and diminishing, running across the hollow towards more stark rocks of the other side. Two small, rapid, intent, dwindling little human figures. The tiny, dark sparks of men. Such specks of gods.

They disappeared, no bigger than stones, behind rocks in shadow. They had gone, it was said, to lay down the snakes before a rock called the snake-shrine, and let them all go free. Free to carry the message and thanks to the dragon-gods who can give and withhold. To carry the human spirit, the human breath, the human prayer, the human gratitude, the human command which had been breathed upon them in the mouths of the priests, transferred into them from those feather-prayersticks which the old wise men swept upon the shoulders of the young, snake-bearing men, to carry this back, into the vaster, dimmer, inchoate regions where the monsters of rain and wind alternated in beneficence and wrath. Carry the human prayer and will-power into the holes of the winds, down into the octopus heart of the rain-source. Carry the corn-meal which the women had scattered, back to that terrific, dread, and causeful dark sun which is at the earth's core, that which sends us corn out of the earth's nearness, sends us food or death, according to our strength of vital purpose, our power of sensitive will, our courage.

It is a battle, a wrestling all the time. The Sun, the nameless Sun, source of all things, which we call sun because the other name is too fearful, this, this vast dark protoplasmic sun from which issues all that feeds our life, this original One is all the time willing and unwilling. Systole, diastole, it pulses its willingness and its unwillingness that we should live and move on, from being to being, manhood to further manhood. Man, small, vulnerable man, the farthest adventurer from the dark heart of the first of suns, into the cosmos of creation. Man, the last god won into existence. And all the time, he is sustained and threated, menaced and sustained from the Source, the innermost sun-dragon. And all the time, he must submit and he must conquer. Submit to the strange beneficence from the Source, whose ways are past finding out. And conquer the strange malevolence of the Source, which is past comprehension also.

For the great dragons from which we draw our vitality are all the time willing and unwilling that we should have being. Hence only the heroes snatch manhood, little by little, from the strange den of the Cosmos.

Man, little man, with his consciousness and his will, must both submit to the great origin-powers of his life, and conquer them. Conquered by man who has overcome his fears, the snakes must go back into the earth with his messages of tenderness, of request, and of power. They go back as rays of love to the dark heart of the first of suns. But they go back also as arrows shot clean by man's sapience and courage, into the resistant, malevolent heart of the earth's oldest, stubborn core. In the core of the first of suns, whence man draws his vitality, lies poison as bitter as the rattlesnake's. This poison man must overcome, he must be master of its issue. Because from the first of suns come travelling the rays that make men strong and glad and gods who can range between the known and the unknown. Rays that quiver out of the earth as serpents do, naked with vitality. But each ray charged with poison for the unwary, the irreverent, and the cowardly. Awareness, wariness, is the first virtue in primitive man's morality. And his awareness must travel back and forth, back and forth, from the darkest origins out to the brightest edifices of creation.

And amid all its crudity, and the sensationalism which comes chiefly out of the crowd's desire for thrills, one cannot help pausing in reverence before the delicate, anointed bravery of the snake-priests (so called), with the snakes.

They say the Hopis have a marvellous secret cure for snakebites. They say the bitten are given an emetic drink, after the dance, by the old women, and that they must lie on the edge of the cliff and vomit, vomit, vomit. I saw none of this. The two snake-men who ran down into the shadow came soon running up again, running all the while, and steering off at a tangent, ran up the mesa once more, but beyond a deep, impassable cleft. And there, when they had come up to our level, we saw them across the cleft distance washing, brown and naked, in a pool; washing off the paint, the medicine, the ecstasy, to come back into daily life and eat food. Because for two days they had eaten nothing, it was said. And for nine days they had been immersed in the mystery of snakes, and fasting in some measure.

Men who have lived many years among the Indians say they do not believe the Hopi have any secret cure. Sometimes priests do die of bites, it is said. But a rattlesnake secretes his poison slowly. Each time he strikes he loses his venom, until if he strikes several times, he has very little wherewithal to poison a man. Not enough, not half enough to kill. His glands must be very full charged with poison, as they are when he merges from winter-sleep, before he can kill a man outright. And even then, he must strike near some artery.

Therefore, during the nine days of the kiva, when the snakes are bathed and lustrated, perhaps they strike their poison away into some inanimate object. And surely they are soothed and calmed with such things as the priests, after centuries of experience, know how to administer to them.

We dam the Nile and take the railway across America. The Hopi smooths the rattlesnake and carries him in his mouth, to send him back into the dark places of the earth, an emissary to the inner powers.

To each sort of man his own achievement, his own victory, his own conquest. To the Hopi, the origins are dark and dual, cruelty is coiled in the very beginnings of all things, and circle after circle creation emerges towards a flickering, revealed Godhead. With Man as the godhead so far achieved, waveringly and for ever incomplete, in this world.

To us and to the Orientals, the Godhead was perfect to start with, and man makes but a mechanical excursion into a created and ordained universe, an excursion of mechanical achievement, and of yearning for the return to the perfect Godhead of the beginning.

To us, God was in the beginning, Paradise and the Golden Age have been long lost, and all we can do is to win back.

To the Hopi, God is not yet, and the Golden Age lies far ahead. Out of the dragon's den of the cosmos, we have wrested only the beginnings of our being, the rudiments of our Godhead.

Between the two visions lies the gulf of mutual negations. But ours was the quickest way, so we are conquerors for the moment.

The American aborigines are radically, innately religious. The fabric of their life is religion. But their religion is animistic, their sources are dark and impersonal, their conflict with their 'gods' is slow, and unceasing.

This is true of the settled pueblo Indian and the wandering Navajo, the ancient Maya, and the surviving Aztec. They are all involved at every moment, in their old, struggling religion.

Until they break in a kind of hopelessness under our cheerful, triumphant success. Which is what is rapidly happening. The young Indians who have been to school for many years are losing their religion, becoming discontented, bored, and rootless. An Indian with his own religion inside him cannot be bored. The flow of the mystery is too intense all the time, too intense, even, for him to adjust himself to circumstances from the darkest origins out to the brightest edifices of creation.

And amid all its crudity, and the sensationalism which comes chiefly out of the crowd's desire for thrills, one cannot help pausing in reverence before the delicate, anointed bravery of the snake-priests (so called), with the snakes.

They say the Hopis have a marvellous secret cure for snakebites. They say the bitten are given an emetic drink, after the dance, by the old women, and that they must lie on the edge of the cliff and vomit, vomit, vomit. I saw none of this. The two snake-men who ran down into the shadow came soon running up again, running all the while, and steering off at a tangent, ran up the mesa once more, but beyond a deep, impassable cleft. And there, when they had come up to our level, we saw them across the cleft distance washing, brown and naked, in a pool; washing off the paint, the medicine, the ecstasy, to come back into daily life and eat food. Because for two days they had eaten nothing, it was said. And for nine days they had been immersed in the mystery of snakes, and fasting in some measure.

Men who have lived many years among the Indians say they do not believe the Hopi have any secret cure. Sometimes priests do die of bites, it is said. But a rattlesnake secretes his poison slowly. Each time he strikes he loses his venom, until if he strikes several times, he has very little wherewithal to poison a man. Not enough, not half enough to kill. His glands must be very full charged with poison, as they are when he merges from winter-sleep, before he can kill a man outright. And even then, he must strike near some artery.

Therefore, during the nine days of the kiva, when the snakes are bathed and lustrated, perhaps they strike their poison away into some inanimate object. And surely they are soothed and calmed with such things as the priests, after centuries of experience, know how to administer to them.

We dam the Nile and take the railway across America. The Hopi smooths the rattlesnake and carries him in his mouth, to send him back into the dark places of the earth, an emissary to the inner powers.

To each sort of man his own achievement, his own victory, his own conquest. To the Hopi, the origins are dark and dual, cruelty is coiled in the very beginnings of all things, and circle after circle creation emerges towards a flickering, revealed Godhead. With Man as the godhead so far achieved, waveringly and for ever incomplete, in this world.

To us and to the Orientals, the Godhead was perfect to start with, and man makes but a mechanical excursion into a created and ordained universe, an excursion of mechanical achievement, and of yearning for the return to the perfect Godhead of the beginning.

To us, God was in the beginning, Paradise and the Golden Age have been long lost, and all we can do is to win back.

To the Hopi, God is not yet, and the Golden Age lies far ahead. Out of the dragon's den of the cosmos, we have wrested only the beginnings of our being, the rudiments of our Godhead.

Between the two visions lies the gulf of mutual negations. But ours was the quickest way, so we are conquerors for the moment.

The American aborigines are radically, innately religious. The fabric of their life is religion. But their religion is animistic, their sources are dark and impersonal, their conflict with their 'gods' is slow, and unceasing.

This is true of the settled pueblo Indian and the wandering Navajo, the ancient Maya, and the surviving Aztec. They are all involved at every moment, in their old, struggling religion.

Until they break in a kind of hopelessness under our cheerful, triumphant success. Which is what is rapidly happening. The young Indians who have been to school for many years are losing their religion, becoming discontented, bored, and rootless. An Indian with his own religion inside him *cannot* be bored. The flow of the mystery is too intense all the time, too intense, even, for him to adjust himself to circumstances which really are mechanical. Hence his failure. So he, in his great religious struggle for the Godhead of man, falls back beaten. The Personal God who ordained a mechanical cosmos gave the victory to his sons, a mechanical triumph.

Soon after the dance is over, the Navajo begin to ride down the Western trail, into the light. Their women, with velvet bodices and full, full skirts, silver and turquoise tinkling thick on their breasts, sit back on their horses and ride down the steep slope, looking wonderingly around from their pleasant, broad, nomadic, Mongolian faces. And the men, long, loose, thin, long-waisted, with tall hats on their brows and low-sunk silver belts on their hips, come down to water their horses at the spring. We say they look wild. But they have the remoteness of their religion, their animistic vision, in their eyes, they can't see as we see. And they cannot accept us. They stare at us as the coyotes stare at us: the gulf of mutual negation between us.

So in groups, in pairs, singly, they ride silently down into the lower strata of light, the aboriginal Americans riding into their shut-in reservations. While the white Americans hurry back to their motor-cars, and soon the air buzzes with starting engines, like the biggest of rattlesnakes buzzing.

8 - A LITTLE MOONSHINE WITH LEMON

'Ye Gods, he doth bestride the narrow world
Like a Colossus...!'

There is a bright moon, so that even the vines make a shadow, and the Mediterranean has a broad white shimmer between its dimness. By the shore, the lights of the old houses twinkle quietly, and out of the wall of the headland advances the glare of a locomotive's lamps. It is a feast day, St Catherine's Day, and the men are all sitting round the little tables, down below, drinking wine or vermouth.

And what about the ranch, the little ranch in New Mexico? The time is different there: but I too have drunk my glass to St Catherine, so I can't be bothered to reckon. I consider that there, too, the moon is in the south-east, standing, as it were, over Santa Fé, beyond the bend of those mountains of Picoris.

Sono io! say the Italians. I am I! Which sounds simpler than it is.

Because which I am I, after all, now that I have drunk a glass also to St Catherine, and the moon shines over the sea, and my thoughts, just because they are fleetingly occupied by the moon on the Mediterranean, and ringing with the last farewell: *Dunque, Signore! di nuovo*!--must needs follow the moon-track south-west, to the great South-west, where the ranch is.

They say: *in vino veritas*. Bah! They say so much! But in the wine of St Catherine, my little ranch, and the three horses down among the timber. Or if it has snowed, the horses are gone away, and it is snow, and the moon shines on the alfalfa slope, between the pines, and the cabins are blind. There is nobody there. Everything shut up. Only the big pine tree in front of the house, standing still and unconcerned, alive.

Perhaps when I have a *Weh* at all, my *Heimweh* is for the tree in front of the house, the overshadowing tree whose green top one never looks at. But on the trunk one hangs the various odds and ends of iron things. It is so near. One goes out of the door, and the tree-trunk is there, like a guardian angel.

The tree-trunk, and the long work table, and the fence! Then beyond, since it is night, and the moon shines, for me at least, away beyond is a light, at Taos, or at Ranchos de Taos. Here, the castle of Noli is on the western skyline. But there, no doubt it has snowed, since even here the wind is cold. There it has snowed, and the nearly full moon blazes wolf-like, as here it never blazes; risen like a were-wolf over the mountains. So there is a faint hoar shagginess of pine trees, away at the foot of the alfalfa field, and a grey gleam of snow in the night, on the level desert, and a ruddy point of human light, in Ranchos de Taos.

And beyond, you see them even if you don't see them, the circling mountains, since there is a moon.

So, one hurries indoors, and throws more logs on the fire.

One doesn't either. One hears Giovanni calling from below, to say good-night! He is going down to the village for a spell. *Vado giù Signor Lorenzo! Buona notte!*

And the Mediterranean whispers in the distance, a sound like in a shell. And save that somebody is whistling, the night is very bright and still. The Mediterranean, so eternally young, the very symbol of youth! And Italy, so reputedly old, yet for ever so child-like and naïve! Never, never for a moment able to comprehend the wonderful, hoary age of America, the continent of the afterwards.

I wonder if I am here, or if I am just going to bed at the ranch. Perhaps looking in Montgomery Ward's catalogue for something for Christmas, and drinking moonshine and hot water, since it is cold. Go out and look if the chickens are shut up warm: if the horses are in sight: if Susan, the black cow, has gone to her nest among the trees, for the night. Cows don't eat much at night. But Susan will wander in the moon. The moon makes her uneasy. And the horses stamp around the cabins.

In a cold like this, the stars snap like distant coyotes, beyond the moon. And you'll see the shadow of actual coyotes, going across the alfalfa field. And the pine trees make little noises, sudden and stealthy, as if they were walking about. And the place heaves with ghosts. That place, the ranch, heaves with ghosts. But when one has got used to one's own home-ghosts, be they never so many, and so potent, they are like one's own family, but nearer than the blood. It is the ghosts one misses most, the ghosts there, of the Rocky Mountains, that never go beyond the timber and that linger, like the animals, round the water-spring. I know them, they know me: we go well together. But they reproach me for going away. They are resentful too.

Perhaps the snow is in tufts on the greasewood bushes. Perhaps the blue jay falls in a blue metallic cloud out of the pine trees in front of the house, at dawn, in the terrific cold, when the dangerous light comes watchful over the mountains, and touches the desert far-off, far-off, beyond the Rio Grande.

And I, I give it up. There is a choice of vermouth, Marsala, red wine or white. At the ranch, tonight, because it is cold, I should have moonshine, not very good moonshine, but still warming: with hot water and lemon, and sugar, and a bit of cinnamon from one of those little red Schilling's tins. And I should light my little stove in the bedroom, and let it roar a bit, sucking the wind. Then dark to bed, with all the ghosts of the ranch cosily round me, and sleep till the very coldness of my emerged nose wakes me. Waking, I shall look at once through the glass panels of the bedroom door, and see the trunk of the great pine tree, like a person on guard, and a low star just coming over the mountain, very brilliant, like someone swinging an electric lantern.

Si vedrà la primavera.

Fiorann' i mandorlini--

Ah, well, let it be vermouth, since there's no moonshine with lemon and cinnamon. Supposing I called Giovanni, and told him I wanted:

'Un poco di chiar' di luna, con canella e limone...'

Made in the USA
Las Vegas, NV
26 July 2023